SE 28 88			
Sept, 6, 91			

ALL ABOUT LANGUAGE

ALL
ABOUT
LANGUAGE

by MARIO PEI

Decorations by Donat Ivanovsky

J. B. LIPPINCOTT COMPANY
PHILADELPHIA & NEW YORK

ACKNOWLEDGMENT

The author wishes to acknowledge his indebtedness to Vanni Publications, 30 West 12 St., New York 11, for permission to reproduce from his earlier work *The World's Chief Languages* the language maps appearing on pages 57, 59, 95 and 145 of this book.

CONTENTS

Part 1 What Is Language?

Part II How Does Language Work?

Part III Our Language

Part IV Other People's Languages

PART ONE

WHAT IS LANGUAGE?

1 *Why Language?*

ONE OF THE VERY FIRST STORIES YOU COME
across when you open your Bible is that of the Tower of
Babel. Men, says the Bible, had grown very proud—to the
point of believing they were as mighty as God. So they
decided to build a great tower that would reach the sky, as
a token of their might and as an act of defiance to God.

But God quickly proved that He was mightier than they.
Up to this time, men had all lived together in one region of
the earth. Being all of the same family, they spoke the same
language and had no trouble understanding one another.
But now, as they began building their tower, God caused
their tongues to change, so that they no longer spoke the
same way. Soon they found they no longer understood one
another when they talked.

For a time, they tried to go on with their building. But
it didn't work. One man would shout an order or a warning to another in his language, and the other would fail to
understand the warning or to follow out the directions.
Things went topsy-turvy. Pretty soon the work of building had to stop.

The men gathered together and tried to settle their differences. They couldn't even do that. So they wandered off
in different directions, each with his own family, speaking
his own language. The tower that was going to reach the
sky remained unfinished, as a warning to all men that God
was mightier than they.

Today, some people believe that all this happened exactly
as it is told in the Bible, others do not. But whether you

believe it or not, there are two important lessons we can learn from the story of the great Tower of Babel. One of these lessons we shall keep in reserve until we reach the end of our book. The other is that without language there is no understanding among people, and without understanding there is no chance of their being able to work together.

It is a lesson we can figure out for ourselves, even without the story of the Tower. If you come across somebody you like, the first thing you want to do is play with him. So you go up to him and say: "Do you want to play ball?" But he stares at you blankly and says: "*Je ne comprends pas!*" You stare blankly back at him and say: "I don't understand!" (which is exactly what he said to you, only he said it in French).

At this point, you may show him the ball and make signs of catching and throwing. He may get the idea, and join you in a simple game of catch. But now other boys come up, and you want to play baseball. Baseball has a lot of rules, and you try to explain the rules to the others. Half of them speak English like you, and they understand without trouble. The other half speak nothing but French. You can't explain to them by gestures that three strikes is out, or that you have to run to first base after you have batted the ball. So the game you are planning falls through. You have to resign yourself to just plain catch, and pretty soon everyone gets tired and bored and goes home. You are leaving your own Tower of Babel behind you.

Without language, there are plenty of things you can do by yourself. There are even a few simple things you can do with others. But the minute what you want to do gets the least bit involved, you need language to make your meaning clear and get help and cooperation from others. No common language means little or no help or cooperation, and that in turn means that nothing really big or worth-while can get done. Since most of the things connected with our civilization are big, they call for lots of help and cooperation, for the joint efforts of many people, all working intelligently together, each with a clear understanding of what the others are doing, and when, where and how he must come in. The only thing that makes possible our skyscrapers, our airplanes, our machines, is the fact that the many people working on them understand one another. Take away that understanding, and they will all sink back into barbarism or savagery, because the means of transferring their thoughts to one another will be lost.

As we shall find out a little later, there are many ways in which ideas may be transferred from the mind of one man to that of another—writing, pictures, gestures, signs and signals. All of them, in a way, are language. But what first comes to mind when we speak of language is speech—the sounds we make with our mouths and receive through our ears.

We see the mouth and the ears, and so we think of them first when we think of speech. What we do not see (but it has to be there) is the brain that thinks out the message spoken by the mouth, and the other brain that receives and acts upon the message heard by the ear. It doesn't really become language until all four have come into play.

Consider this: you may make nonsense sounds with your mouth; they will be heard by someone else's ear, and transferred to his brain; but they won't mean anything. Why not? Because the first step is missing—your brain wasn't working when you produced the sounds.

If you have a thought, but don't open your mouth to speak it out, only the first step of language is completed. The missing second step blocks out the rest of the process.

Or suppose you think and speak, but the other party doesn't hear you. Steps three and four are out, and there is no real language. If the other person hears, but his brain is asleep, or busy with something else, there is still no real language.

But now suppose you think: "I am going to throw the ball, and Johnny has to catch it!" Then you say to your friend: "Johnny, catch the ball I'm going to throw!" He hears you, and his brain is wide awake. When you throw the ball, he is ready for it. This is true language, with full transfer of meaning from one brain to another, and cooperation between two or more human beings based upon that transfer.

So far, we have been talking about language in terms of working or playing together. Language can also be used as an end in itself. Two people meet. What do they normally do? They talk, even if they have nothing that they want to work on together. They exchange ideas, impressions, information, whether they talk about the weather, what's going on in their homes, clubs or businesses, or on the baseball diamond, or in Washington, or abroad.

Normally, such talk leads to friendliness. It is true that sometimes it may lead to quarrels and fights. But for every time this happens, there are at least a hundred times when the two speakers part better friends than when they started. They know more about each other's problems, hopes and troubles, joys and sorrows, likes and dislikes, and the more they know the friendlier they feel.

Compare this with what would happen if they had no way of communicating their thoughts to each other. They would be suspicious, each one wondering what the other was thinking. If they had to spend a great deal of time together in silence, their suspicions would grow. Each would wonder if the other were plotting to do him some harm when his back was turned. Soon they would get to distrust each other.

So language is probably the greatest breeder of friendliness in the world. Misunderstandings and suspicions are cleared away by it, and people are made aware of the fact that after all they are not so very different from one another as they thought.

Language is what your doctor has to use when you go to him with a complaint; he listens to you as you tell him what's wrong, and then tells you what you should do about it. Language is what your teacher has to use when he or she explains things to you. Language is what your parents, your priest, minister or rabbi use when they try to help you with your problems. Language is what your favorite radio or TV star uses to entertain you; it's what your movie hero uses, so that you may understand what's going on in the picture. It's used by the policeman who guides you across the street, the clerk in the grocery store, the bus driver who takes you to the place where you want to go, the man at the news-stand who sells you the daily paper. In fact, it's used by everybody you know. Imagine all these people, including yourself, suddenly losing the power of speech. Then figure out how much of a role language plays in your life, and just where you would be if it didn't exist.

At this point, you might ask: "Was it always there? If not, when and where did it start?" You'll find some sort of an answer in the next chapter.

There is another question that may come to your mind: "Who makes language?" The answer is simple: you, and millions of others like you.

Language, like thinking, is one activity in which practically everybody shares. The number of people who don't think, outside of infants and idiots, is very small (and even here there is a good deal of doubt; infants and idiots, according to many scientists, do plenty of thinking, along their own lines). The number of people who don't speak is even smaller. Practically everybody speaks, and by the very fact that people use language, they make language.

For the most part, people take language as it is handed down to them. Children learn to speak from their parents and elders, and follow the pattern of sounds and words they hear, just as they follow the pattern of ideas their elders present. But often enough, they make little changes—in the sounds, in the words, in the meanings of the words, in the way the words are put together. For the most part, these little changes don't get beyond the person making them. But sometimes the changes are liked by those who hear them, as happened when somebody thought of "hot dog" in connection with what had been known before as a "frankfurter." The change spreads, and is finally taken up by all the speakers. It gets into the newspapers, the books, the radio and TV programs, finally into the dictionary. By the time this happens, the person who first made the little change may have forgotten that he was responsible for it. Yet he, in that particular sound or word or usage, made the language! That person may very well be you.

Should you deliberately set about trying to "make the language"? I would hardly advise it. People who try too hard often set themselves apart from others and get laughed at. On the other hand, if you should happen to come out with something that other people seem to like, don't be too ashamed of it. Others have done it before you.

But there is another, more important way in which you can "make the language." It is by using your own good sense of choice as to whether you will accept or not a new sound, word or meaning suggested by someone else. The final decision as to whether a change gets into the language rests not with the one who makes the change, but with the hundreds and thousands and millions who are asked to accept it. Here every one of us has a chance to "make the language," to take or refuse what is offered in the way of change. You can use your power of choice even in the case of the older sounds and words and meanings. Many of these, which at one time were part of the language, dropped out because the speakers chose not to use them any longer.

Don't be afraid to exercise your power of choice. If you prefer "telephone" to "phone," or "greatly" to "very much," don't be afraid to use them. It's your language as much as anyone else's. At the same time, try to have a good reason for your choice, because language is one of the finest products of man's intelligence, and should be intelligently employed and intelligently changed. Above all, don't be afraid of language. It's there for you to use. It's meant to help you, not to hinder you. It will serve you at work or at play, in everything you do; it will make friends for you; it will add to the enjoyment of every minute of your life. It carries your ideas to others, as well as their ideas to you. It is your representative. It is you. Speak up!

2 How Did Speech Begin?

TO MOST PEOPLE, LANGUAGE MEANS SPEECH.
The word *language* itself comes from Latin *lingua*,
"tongue," and its original meaning is "that which is produced with the tongue."

But there is another meaning to "language"—what carries
a message from one human mind to another. This defini-
tion makes language far more inclusive. If you accept it,
language is not only speech; it is also writing, pictures, symbols that catch the eye, like red and green traffic lights; gestures made with the hands and expressions of the face or
eyes; sounds made not with the voice, but by mechanical
means, like a fire alarm or a doorbell. Often several of these
messages are combined to convey a single meaning, as when
you hold out your hand, smile, and say "Shake!"—all at the
same time. But we shall speak later of the forms of language
that are not speech.

Speech is by far the most common and widespread form
of language, so that to many people language and speech
are one and the same thing.

Did human beings always possess the power of speech?
If not, when and how did they acquire it? Are human beings the only ones to have it?

These are questions that have long troubled the people
who work in the field of language and try to find out all
about it. You have no sure answer to these questions, and
neither have they.

All they can tell you is that human beings seem to have had the power of speech as far back as history can trace them; that animals, while they can make certain limited sounds and at times give them certain limited meanings, cannot be said to possess speech in the same sense that humans possess it. Animals, furthermore, have been producing the selfsame sounds as far back as man's memory can reach, while the speech of human beings is forever changing.

The question is still unanswered whether animals of certain species manage to communicate with one another by means other than sound. Some scientists claim that ants and other insects exchange messages by means of their feelers, that bees emit certain meaningful odors perceptible to other bees, or dance in their hives in ways that convey a meaning to their fellow-bees. But all this is still doubtful.

For what concerns animal sounds, all the proof we have points in the same direction—that dogs have been barking, cats meowing, lions roaring, lambs bleating, horses neighing, donkeys braying in precisely the same way since they first came to the notice of human beings. The variety of feelings and emotions that a dog can display with his bark is quite limited. He can express joy, fear, hunger, and perhaps half a dozen other basic feelings with his voice. Beyond that, he cannot go. He cannot tell a connected story. He cannot "speak."

Even birds that imitate human sounds, like the parrot or the mynah-bird, are restricted in the number of sounds and words they can utter, and seem for the most part unable to link a given sound or word with a specific meaning.

The speech-feature of the human being lies not so much in his ability to produce sounds, as in his mental capacity to link the sounds with meanings which are accepted by other human beings so that there is a real transfer of thought from one mind to another. It is only in this sense that you have real speech and real language. The mere capacity to make nonsense-sounds is not language. Neither is it real language when the sounds have meaning only to the one who makes them. Newborn babies make sounds which may have a meaning to them, but which their elders do not understand. Insane people sometimes make up words which they alone can understand. This is not language.

Language actually begins when two or more human beings decide that a certain sound, or set of sounds, shall have the same meaning to both or all of them. At this point, a language is born.

Granted this, the people who make it their business to study language have gone into various suppositions as to how the first language or languages may have arisen.

One plausible idea is that two primitive human beings, hearing the same natural sound, may have set out together to imitate it, agreeing on the imitation, then agreeing that the source of the natural sound should be called by their agreed-upon imitation. For instance, two men listening to a dog barking may have agreed on "bow-wow" as the closest possible imitation of the dog's bark, then gone on to designate that particular dog, and finally all dogs, as "bow-wow."

Along with this, there may have been common acceptance of certain exclamations to indicate certain feelings or emotions: "Ouch!" as a general indication of pain, "Oh!" of surprise, "Ah!" of satisfaction, "Awrk!" of anger, "Ugh!" of bodily exertion.

Then may have come the standardization of certain sounds to indicate certain actions or qualities, particularly those involving some natural sound that could be somehow imitated, like "crush" and "smash" and "gurgle."

If all this is true, the first thing that comes to our mind

is that the process of creating a language must have been a very slow and painful one, stretching out over thousands, perhaps millions of years, with one set of speakers advancing just a little bit beyond the ones that came before them, until what had at first been little more than a series of grunts and groans and animal noises turned into a real language.

The next thing we realize is that if language grew up, as we suppose, by mutual agreement, it is not surprising that there are so many different languages in the world. Two speakers in one valley, hearing the dog's bark, may have agreed on "bow-wow," but two other speakers in the next valley, hearing the same sound, may have taken it as "woof-woof." Right there you have the beginning of your language differences. The dog would be "bow-wow" to one set of speakers, "woof-woof" to the other. The "Ouch!" of pain of one group might have been "Ow!" to another and "Ahee!" to a third. This is borne out by the fact that these differences actually appear in the various languages today. An American imitates the dog as "bow-wow" or "woof-woof," but a Frenchman imitates the dog by saying *oua-oua*, while an Italian says *bu-bu*. The American "ouch" of pain is not used by the Spaniards, who say *ay*.

Another and very important feature of language that we notice is the absolute need for agreement between at least two people. If one speaker insisted on his own "bow-wow" and the other on "woof-woof," there would be no getting together of the minds, and consequently no language. This principle is of importance even today. If you are using a language that says "dog," and find yourself among people who say *chien*, you will neither understand nor be understood. There will be no transfer of ideas between you and the people around you. For the time being, until you learn their sound-and-meaning combinations, or go back to the people who use the same combinations you use, you may be said to have no language.

The picture we have drawn of the origin of language is interesting, and may be true. Or it may not be. Why can't we be sure? Because the earliest speakers did not leave us any phonograph records (the phonograph record, which takes down sounds so that they can be repeated at will, goes back only to the last part of the nineteenth century). What records did they leave us? Pictures, scribbled on the walls of caves (but these do not really prove they spoke); then, much later, written messages, which really put down speech in lasting form. But before human beings invented writing, they had been speaking for many thousands of years, slowly and painfully building up their speech, and of that long building-up process there is no record. So we can only guess at what went on.

By the time the first written records appeared, the spoken language had already been built up to a very satisfactory stage—that much the written records show us. The earliest written records of a language are in Sumerian, a tongue spoken in Mesopotamia (what is today Iraq) about six thousand years ago. Six thousand years seems a long time; yet it is practically certain that human beings had been speaking for many times that number of years before they got around to recording their speech on stone, or bricks, or clay tablets.

Among the oldest languages of which we have written records, besides Sumerian, are Akkadian (the language of the Babylonians and Assyrians), Egyptian, Hebrew, Chinese and Sanskrit. Greek and Latin came much later, within the first thousand years before Christ. Most of the tongues spoken today are very young indeed, having appeared after the time of Christ, within the last two thousand years. Many of them, however, were probably spoken long before, but simply did not get into written form.

The theory we have outlined of the beginning of speech is only one of many. There are some who believe that the human race arose in a single spot, and developed at first a single language, and that later, as human beings wandered off in different directions, this once common language changed more and more, until it finally developed into the vast number of different tongues spoken today. There is no doubt that this took place in part, because many languages today show a common beginning, with evidence of differences arising in the course of wanderings of people who at one time lived in one spot and used the same language. But whether *all* languages can be traced back to a single one, and *all* people to a single locality, is very much in doubt.

Yet some linguists are fascinated by the similarities they find in certain words in the most remote corners of the earth and among people of the most different racial stocks. Words like "daddy" and "mama" appear in many languages, with much the same meaning they hold for us. The Chinese word for "mother," for instance, is *ma*, even though Chinese is not supposed to have any connection with the languages of the West. The use of "puss" or some similar sound (*bis, pss, pusei, piso*) to call a cat is found in most parts of Europe, as well as in North Africa, Arabia and southern India.

Will we ever get to find out about the real starting-point of language? The chances are we won't. The only proof we can rely on is that of writing. But speech came long before writing, and of ancient speech there is no record. We can only guess.

3 Could We Get Along Without Speech?

BEFORE GOING FURTHER, WE SHOULD PER-
haps cast a glance at all those systems of communication in
which speech plays no part. First and foremost among
them, of course, is writing. But writing, in modern society,
has become such an important and widespread means of
getting your ideas across to others that we can reserve an
entire chapter for it.

It was not always so, however. Time was, and not too
long ago, when most people did not know how to read and
write. Curious reminders of that not very distant past are
the barber-shop poles and the cigar-store Indians. They
served to notify people who could not read of what goods
or services they could get in those shops.

If we go back far enough, there was a time when writing
had not yet been invented. Yet people managed to get
messages through to one another without speech even then.
Today, they still manage to convey messages without either
speech or writing.

Consider, for instance, your system of traffic lights. At
a given street intersection there is no policeman, no written
sign. But the light turns red, and the motorists stop. Then
it turns green, and they start moving once more. That light
is just as full of meaning as though the words "Stop" and
"Go" were spoken or written.

Signals recognized by the eye can take many forms.
There are signal fires and smoke signals (the latter were

16

much used by the Plains Indians). There are signal flags, used especially at sea to convey all sorts of complicated messages. There is the heliograph, that device used by the U. S. Navy to catch and reflect the sun's rays into the eyes of men miles away, and spell out a message to them.

Then there are thousands of ear-signals. The whistle of a policeman or referee, the siren of an ambulance or fire engine, the bell at your door or in the classroom, all convey messages as clear as though they were spoken. Usually it is a single, simple message that is conveyed to the listener. But not always. The natives of the Congo, in Africa, have a tom-tom jungle "telephone" by means of which they are able to send long and complicated messages. One variety of this tom-tom consists of a section of hardwood log about five feet long and two feet in diameter, hollowed out, but with the ends filled in, with a slit in the top and the walls so graduated that striking the side of the slot away from the operator gives a low tone and the near side a high tone. It is played with two sticks about a foot long, to the ends of which are fastened latex balls. The succession of high and low tones spells out messages, which in some cases seem to imitate the pitch of the voice in native words, in others are simply based on a previous understanding, like our own Morse Code *SOS*, which is universally accepted as indicating distress.

The Morse Code, based on dots and dashes, or long and short buzzes when it comes over telegraph wires, spells out letters of the alphabet which in turn are combined into words and sentences. This brings it close to writing. On the other hand, long and short toots from a locomotive stand not for letters, but for complete messages. Three short toots and one long blast tell the flagman to protect the front of the train; if reversed, to proceed to the rear;

three shorts mean "I'm going to back up"; two longs mean "I'm releasing the brakes; let's go!"

Other examples of sound language not based on speech are the Army bugle calls, over forty in number, each one of which has a different meaning which the soldiers must learn, and the whistling language of the Canary Islands, used by the natives to convey messages across the deep gorges where the sound of the voice does not carry. Nor should we forget our conventional way of indicating approval by clapping the hands and disapproval by hissing.

Coming back to eye-signals, the Incas of Peru, who had not developed a system of writing, had a way of conveying messages by sending swift runners with knotted ropes from one part of their empire to another. The kind of knots in the ropes, along with the colors of the ropes themselves, would tell the story.

Other primitive peoples used notched sticks to carry their thoughts at a distance. These methods of communication come perhaps closer to primitive forms of writing than to substitutes for speech, but since writing itself is a substitute for speech, it does not make much difference.

One great and widespread means of communication which probably came long before speech, but which still accompanies it, is gesture. Gesture is usually made with the hands, sometimes the arms, but practically all parts of the body can enter it, particularly the face. One might even say that all facial expressions, smiles, frowns, pouts, etc., are a form of gesture. Everything you do that is perceptible to the eye carries a meaning, and to that extent is language.

Here again, as in the case of sounds, we find differences. Gesture may be very simple and elementary, conveying a single, simple emotion; or it may be turned into a thorough-going, complicated system that comes close enough to a spoken language to be able to replace it.

Ushers in large theaters have a whole set of gestures which they use to indicate to each other at a distance what seats are available and where. Traffic policemen, baseball umpires, football referees, TV directors, all have sets of gestures that carry limited but specific meanings (on TV, for instance, a gesture of cutting the throat, made by the director to the actor, means "Time's up! Finish your speech at once!") These are languages, but they are limited in scope and restricted to a single field.

But there are gesture languages that are unrestricted and complete. Our American Indians, particularly the Plains tribes, had a system of gestures or sign-language that enabled members of different tribes, speaking totally different languages, to communicate with one another, and also with the white man, without the least trouble and on all sorts of topics. Here are a few samples of this sign-language. To indicate that he was feeling sad, the Indian would point to his heart, then draw his hand down and away in the direction of the ground: "My heart is low" would be a literal spoken translation. If he wanted to indicate "autumn," he would first make the sign for tree: open left hand, thumb and fingers spread, back outward, about the height of the shoulder, moved slowly upward, to indicate growth; then the sign for a falling leaf, drawing the hand down with a fluttering motion: "When trees lose their leaves."

This Indian sign-language is so effective that it has been adopted, with some changes, by the International Boy Scouts, who use it at their jamborees, where Scouts of different nationalities and languages come together. The deaf-mute language is even more thorough, and it is said that as many as three hundred thousand different meanings can be expressed with it.

Gesture language almost certainly came before spoken language. It works well. It can be used among people of different nations. Why, then, did not mankind evolve a universal sign language in the place of many spoken tongues?

There are a few good reasons. Sign language requires visibility. You cannot talk by gestures around a corner, or where any object, such as a door, stands between you and the person you are "speaking" to. You cannot sign-talk in the dark. The spoken language, on the other hand, can be used in the dark and around obstacles. Gesture language ties up your hands. While you are using it, you cannot do anything else with your hands; but speech permits you to work and talk at the same time. Sign-language ties up your eyes; spoken language allows you to listen and at the same time look elsewhere.

Last of all, sign-language is not any more truly international than speech, unless you make it so. We are often struck by the strangeness of gestures employed by foreigners, while they find our own gestures equally strange. If you hold your hand out palm upward, then bend your fingers several times toward yourself, in American gesture-language you indicate that you want the other person to come toward you; but to a Frenchman or an Italian that gesture would mean "good-bye." The reverse gesture, with the palm of the hand down, would mean "good-bye" to us and "come here" to them. The only parts of sign-language that are truly universal (and even here there is some doubt) are those basic and usually unconscious facial expressions that show fear, dislike, pleasure, disappointment, etc.—the smile, the frown, the pout, and a few more. Other gestures, especially those made with the hands, depend for their understanding on exactly the same thing that spoken words depend on—a previous arrangement on the part of two or more people by which they agree that the particular sign shall have a particular meaning.

So we are pretty much back where we started. Speech, as we have developed it, is the best, simplest, easiest, most convenient way of transferring our thoughts to others. Other ways of communication can help, or be used on special occasions, but they, like speech, have to depend on previous arrangement that a certain sign, visible to the eye or audible to the ear, shall carry a certain meaning. Without this previous arrangement, everything falls into confusion, and the real purpose of language (any kind of language) fails.

The real purpose of language is to carry meaning—to transfer thought from one human brain to another. If language doesn't do this, it isn't language—it is just sound, or light, or meaningless gesture.

Would it be worth while to have a system by which the same symbol, or sound, or gesture, would mean the same thing to all men? It probably would.

4 *The Art of Writing*

THERE IS ONE MORE FORM OF LANGUAGE which mankind has worked out at the cost of infinite pain and trouble, long after having developed gestures, symbols and speech. It has the advantage of being permanent and lasting, so that the messages it conveys do not disappear as soon as they are produced, but can be understood at a great distance, and from era to era. This form of language is writing, one of the youngest among the basic means of communication, but also one which no civilized group of men today could do without. When you stop to consider how much information comes to you in written form, rather than in speech, gestures or symbols, you will at once realize its importance, and see why we devote all of one chapter to it.

There is little doubt that writing started with the drawing of pictures to tell a story or convey a message. Forty or fifty thousand years ago, primitive men in France, Spain and North Africa depicted on the walls of their caves hunting scenes designed to record their achievements in the chase of large animals. The art of picture writing later was developed to a high degree by some American Indian tribes, who would inscribe on the bark of trees complete pictorial histories of their expeditions, somewhat similar to a comic strip account, with the characters appearing over and over again as their actions unfolded.

The Sumerians in Mesopotamia, the Egyptians in the valley of the Nile, and the ancient Chinese, all developed full systems of picture writing, but with widely different tools.

The Sumerians, and the Babylonians and Assyrians after them, pressed wedge-shaped instruments into wet clay tablets that later hardened, giving rise to the cuneiform or "wedge-shaped" system of writing. The Egyptians carved their hieroglyphs on stone with chisels and hammers (the word "hieroglyph" means "sacred stone"). Later they discovered that they could paint with brushes on a dried reed called papyrus, from which the word "paper" comes. But actual paper as we know it, made from old rags steeped in a liquid, ground and pressed, first arose in China. In the countries of Europe, stone inscriptions like the Egyptian ones and wax tablets written upon with a sharp instrument called stylus (from which we get the word "style") were soon supplemented by dried sheepskins, or parchment, inscribed with a goose-quill, or pen (*pinna*, from which the word "pen" comes, in Latin means feather), steeped in ink (the word "ink" comes from *encaustum*, "burned out"; any charred and blackened substance, diluted in water, would produce a black liquid suitable for leaving marks on a parchment). Chinese-invented paper did not spread to Europe until less than a thousand years ago.

The very first writings consisted merely of pictures. Sumerians, Egyptians and Chinese at first developed a set of pictures to represent visible objects—a round disk for "sun," a crescent for "moon," a trunk with branches for "tree," a trunk with two legs for "man," and so forth. This produced a very rough and unsatisfactory system of writing. First of all, it gave signs for objects, but not for actions, like "go" and "eat," or for qualities, like "good" and "bad." Secondly, not all things can be pictured; what to do about "east" or "west," "justice" or "happiness"? Lastly, picture writing has no connection with the sounds of the spoken language. This is partly an advantage, because all will be able to recognize the written symbol regardless of what spoken word they use for the object; but it is also a disadvantage, because it provides no link between speech and writing.

The early writers went cleverly to work on these problems. They contrived figures which would indicate those spoken words which their picture system lacked. The pictures of a man in motion, for instance, could be used for "go"; a hand bringing food to a mouth would indicate "eat." For "good," the Chinese worked out a combination of "woman" and "child"; for "east," they combined "sun" and "tree" (the sun rising over the trees). Once this combination process had started, there was no limit to it. "Green" and "year," themselves combined characters, were recombined to form "youth"; four combined characters, standing for "faith," "piety," "temperance" and "justice," were recombined to produce "virtue." The Chinese still use this system today, having developed it to the point of producing some 40,000 combined characters out of a few hundred original pictures of visible objects.

The advantage of this system is that anyone can use it, regardless of the language he speaks. As a matter of fact, the Chinese use many different dialects, and a person from one part of China may not at all understand the speech of the native of another province. But the writing is the same. It does not represent sounds, but objects and ideas. It works out like our numeral system. The figure 10 will have the same meaning in all the countries of the west, even though we say "ten," the French *dix*, the Russians *desyat'*.

But the drawbacks are many. Think of having to learn to read and write not an alphabet of twenty-six letters, but a set of forty thousand different symbols! Actually, only about four thousand are in common everyday use, but even so, it takes the Chinese schoolboy many long and weary years to learn them.

In the west, things went differently. For a time, the ancient peoples worked on with pictures and combinations of pictures. Then it occurred to a Semitic tribe, related to the present-day Hebrews, to link some of these symbols not to ideas, but to the sounds of the spoken tongue. This produced a revolution in writing. There was a symbol for "house," which in the spoken Semitic language was *beth*. The symbol looked pretty much like a simple house—floor, roof and wall, with an opening on the left. Instead of using this symbol to represent the idea of "house," or the entire spoken word *beth*, they agreed to let it stand merely for the first sound of the word *beth*, the sound of *b*. Other symbols were similarly set apart to represent a single sound. After many tries, they finally came out with a set of symbols each one of which stood for just one sound. The number of objects, actions, qualities and ideas is almost endless, and so would be the number of symbols used to represent each one individually. But the number of separate sounds in any given language is quite small—somewhere between twenty and sixty. So, if you have symbols, or letters, that represent sounds instead of objects and ideas, you are cutting down your system of writing to the point where you can easily manage it. The same sounds appear in *but* and *tub*, only in a different order. If you insist on portraying whole words or ideas, you will have to use two entirely different symbols for *but* and *tub*. But if you portray sounds, the same three letters, differently arranged, will serve for both.

So the early Semites brought down the art of writing to something that could be handled with relative ease. What they finally came out with was an alphabet of twenty-two letters. The name "alphabet" itself, though, shows that it got its start in picture writing, for *alpha* goes back to *aleph*, Semitic for "ox" (the letter A was originally the picture of the head of an ox), and *bet* is *beth*, or "house."

From the Semites, the alphabet spread to the Greeks, then to the Romans. Both Greeks and Romans made changes in the form of the letters and added to their number. It is the Roman form of the alphabet that most western languages use today, though each language gives it its own peculiar twist. Some languages use special marks over or beneath some letters to indicate some of their own sounds. In French, for example, you will find accent-marks over vowels (*é, è, ê*) and an occasional cedilla under a *c* (*ç*); in Spanish you will find a tilde over an *n* (*ñ*); in German, umlaut marks over *a, o, u* (*ä, ö, ü*). You will also find combinations of letters that are strange to you, like *aa* in Dutch, Danish and Finnish, *cs* in Hungarian, *szcz* in Polish.

The original Semitic alphabet ran from right to left. Semitic languages in use today, like Hebrew and Arabic, still use that arrangement. The early Greeks who first borrowed the Semitic alphabet were uncertain as to the direction they should give their writing, and for a time ran their lines alternately from right to left, then from left to right, then from right to left again. They called this way of writing "as the ox ploughs." Finally they fixed on the left to right arrangement as the more satisfactory, and passed it on to the Romans, who in turn passed it on to us. The Greeks continued to use their own version of the alphabet (American fraternities and sororities use Greek letters in their names). They also in part passed it on to the Russians and some other Slavic peoples, in an alphabet that is called Cyrillic after one of the two Greek bishops, Cyril and

Methodius, who Christianized the Slavs and taught them to write.

The Anglo-Saxons who were the ancestors of the English at first used an alphabet of their own called Runic, the letters of which were supposed to have magic powers, and which they therefore carved at every opportunity on their weapons and tools. It seems that the Runic alphabet, which was also used by the ancient Scandinavians, was borrowed from an early Greek version, but of this we are not altogether sure. When the Anglo-Saxons and Scandinavians were converted to Christianity, they dropped Runic and adopted the Roman alphabet.

Today, the civilized world is somewhat unevenly divided between the alphabetic system based on sound, originally devised by the Semites, and the old system based on picture writing evolved by the Chinese. The latter passed on their method, with certain changes, to the Japanese, and since the Chinese and Japanese account for well over half a billion people, it may be said, roughly, that one-fourth of the world's population gets along with the old picture-and-idea writing. The other three-fourths use alphabets in which the written symbol is linked not with an object or idea, but with a spoken sound.

Chinese and Japanese printed pages usually are arranged in vertical columns running from top to bottom, and read one after the other from right to left. But they will often also write as we do, horizontally and from left to right.

Among the alphabets, the closest to the original Semitic is the Hebrew, which is used also in Yiddish. Then comes the Arabic, used by all Arab peoples and spreading out, with minor changes, to most nations whose religion is the Moslem, like Iran and Pakistan. Europe and the Western

Hemisphere are generally served by the Roman alphabet, but the Greeks still use their ancient Greek letters, and the Russians, Serbs and Bulgars use Cyrillic. India, Ceylon, Burma, Thailand have very numerous alphabets which are distantly derived, with many and startling changes, from the Semitic.

The nations that use alphabets based on sounds have not altogether given up the system of symbols based on ideas. Consider, first and foremost, our system of numbers, which is international, though the numbers are read differently. We also have many limited languages of written symbols: the system of musical notes, the symbols used in chemistry, in mathematics, in astronomy, in dozens of other fields. One of the most recent "languages" to come to public notice is the "snow language" of Canada, used also by Switzerland, Scandinavia, Japan, and parts of South America, where heavy snows are a common problem. A series of circles indicates rounded grains of snow, but a series of squares means that the grains have crystal facets; a straight line with a broken line over it means "film crust," but two straight lines, one above the other, means "wind crust."

Consider, too, all that part of our written language which is symbolical of things other than sounds: capitals, italics, periods, commas, question and exclamation marks, quotes, paragraphs. These devices may be said, if you are reading out loud, to represent directions, but if you are reading silently they are mere indicators of how the thought is to be broken up or interpreted. So they are primarily thought-symbols rather than sound-symbols, and link our way of writing with that of the Chinese.

In countries like ours, practically everybody goes to school and learns to read and write. This, unfortunately, is still not true of many parts of the world, where there is much illiteracy. Less than two centuries ago, only twenty per cent of our American population could read and write. Today, the man who cannot read and write is rare. A great deal of our greatness as a nation has been built on the fact that our people are educated and literate.

The man who cannot read and write is shut off from the world of books, magazines and newspapers. He cannot even read a road-sign or a direction. He cannot communicate with his fellow-man at a distance, save by telephone or telegraph. He cannot engage in work, save of a purely manual kind. He is indeed handicapped.

Yet in many areas of the earth only one person out of two, or five, or ten, or even fifty, is able to read and write. There is still much work to be done in this field.

5 What Is Language Made Up Of?

WITH ALL THE IMPORTANCE THAT THE written language has taken on, particularly in the last two hundred years, speech still remains the basic way of transferring our thoughts to our fellow-man. Here the situation is different. There is no human group, no matter how backward or illiterate, that does not possess speech. Nor is the speech restricted to mere grunts and groans just because the population is backward or illiterate. On the contrary, we find that some groups that have no written language often have a very highly developed spoken tongue.

We can therefore turn our spotlight back again to speech, the most perfect and universal form of language, and the greatest by far of all the means by which human beings transmit their thoughts, feelings and intentions to one another.

The first thing that strikes us about speech is that it consists of sounds. The sounds seem to issue from your mouth, but if you observe carefully you will notice that many other parts of the body enter into sound-production. The lungs supply the air for the sounds, and act as a bellows. If you place your fingers to the sides of your throat you will detect a vibration that occurs as you speak; what vibrates is the vocal cords inside your throat. The air pushed out by your lungs resounds in your throat, or your nose, or your mouth, all of which act as sounding-boards. The tongue plays a prominent part in speech, by touching the teeth, or the gums, or the palate, and either forming a complete barrier which is quickly released so that the air comes out in a puff, or shaping a narrow opening through which the air is gradually forced out. Sometimes the lips do this instead of the tongue. According to the way you use your lungs, throat, vocal cords, tongue and lips, you produce different sounds. These sounds are carried on air-waves to the ears of your listener. There they are transformed into a series of electrical impulses that finally reach his brain. If there is a previous understanding between you and him that a certain sequence of sounds shall have a certain meaning, that meaning gets across from your brain to his.

You think of a cat. In your mind, the animal is associated with the word "cat," which is made up of three sounds coming one after the other. If you produce only one of these sounds, your listener will know that you have produced a sound, but he will be unable to give it any meaning. It is only when you put together the three sounds, c-a-t, that you will get a message across to him. C-a-t means something to him and to you both. It is a word, and a word is a definite succession of sounds which the speakers of a language have agreed shall have a definite meaning.

This, however, still doesn't tell your listener too much. He hears "cat," and he figures out that your mind is concerned with a cat. But that is all he knows. He still doesn't know whether the cat you have in mind is white, black, gray or brindled, whether it is small or large, whether it is standing, sitting, lying, walking or running.

But now, along with the word "cat," you produce other words. You say "See the big white cat running up the street!" Now your listener has a complete message. Even if he doesn't see the animal, he has a description of the cat, a statement about what the cat is doing and where. He has a sentence, which is a complete message. Of course, the message can be made longer and more complete. You can give the entire history and background of the cat, state to whom it belongs, what it was doing before it started running, what it will probably do later on, and so forth. But with your first sentence, you have already gotten a complete meaning across to your listener.

Speech is made up of sentences. Sentences are made up words. Words are made up of sounds. It is quite possible to have a sentence made up of only one word, as when you say "Stop!" It is even possible for a word to consist of only one sound, as when you say "a" in "a house." But for the most part words consist of several connected sounds, and sentences of several connected words. The main purpose of speech is to get meanings across. Sentences, words, sounds are the tools by which this is done.

There is one more thing that enters the picture of speech. If instead of saying "See the big white cat running up the street," you say "See the big white *cats* running up the street," you give your listener a somewhat different idea. Now he sees not one, but several large white cats. How did you bring about this change? By adding the sound of *-s* to *cat*. The addition of the *-s* turns *cat* from one to more than one. The *-s* all by itself would have no meaning, but when added to *cat* it changes its meaning. The *-s* is an ending whose sole job it is to add to the simple idea of *cat* the additional idea of "more than one."

So we have four basic elements in speech—sounds, words, the arrangement of words into groups or sentences, and endings or other changes in words (like the change of *a* to *e* in "man," "men") that add something to the original meaning of words.

The first three elements, sounds, words and sentences,

appear in all spoken languages. Endings or other changes within a word appear in a great many languages, but not in all. Some languages, like Chinese, never make any change within or at the end of a word. Other languages, like Latin or Russian, use far more such changes than we do in English.

All languages have sounds. Do all languages have the same sounds? Not at all. The number of possible sounds that you can produce with your throat, nose, tongue, palate, teeth, lips has never been counted, but it runs into the hundreds, and probably the thousands. No one language uses more than a small fraction of all these possible sounds, usually no fewer than twenty and no more than sixty. Even where two languages use what seems to be the same sound, there are almost always small differences that a trained ear can catch. Take, for instance, the sound of *t*. You produce it by putting the tip of your tongue against the ridge of your upper gums, without touching the teeth. A Frenchman produces it by putting the tip of his tongue square against the back of the upper teeth. What you hear is almost the same sound, but not quite.

When a baby begins to speak, he imitates his elders. He tries to produce the same sounds he hears them producing. Sometimes he makes funny mistakes, but eventually, by listening and repeating over and over again, he learns to produce those thirty or forty or fifty sounds just as they do. After a time, those thirty or forty or fifty tongue-and-lip-and-mouth positions become natural to him, and all other positions unnatural and difficult. So, when he starts learning another language in high school, the sounds of the new language seem strange and hard. Actually, they aren't. If he had started with that language when he was a baby, those sounds would have become easy and natural for him, and the sounds of English would be the hard ones. There seems to be almost no limit to the number of sounds one can learn to produce easily and naturally if he starts early enough, and there are many people who, having heard and spoken two or more languages from the time they were babies, speak them all like natives.

But by the time you are ten, your habits are set, and it is difficult to change them. People who start learning another language after that age find it hard to imitate the mouth-positions of the foreign language, and often substitute the nearest sounds of their own language for them. That is why an American pronouncing a French word that has a *t* forgets or neglects to make the little shift in the position of the tongue that would give him a real French *t*, and pronounces the word with an English *t* instead. Since the two sounds are close, he will be readily understood by the Frenchman, but the latter will know at once he is a foreigner. He is speaking French with an English accent. The Frenchman, on the other hand, will find it hard to adjust his mouth to the position of *th* in *this* (a sound that never appears in French), and will tend to replace it with the nearest French sound, *z*. He says "zis book" and gives himself away.

There is no sound in any foreign language that you cannot master if you work at it long and hard enough, and many people learn to speak another language like natives even after the age of ten. But it takes a lot of effort.

All languages have words. Most often the words correspond; a word like "water" or "sun," for instance, will be found in practically any language. In a good many cases, however, there are differences. If one were to ask "How do you say *man* in Latin?"—the answer would have to be that there are two words, *vir* and *homo*, the first to be used in connection with an individual (as in "This man is strong"), the latter having rather the meaning of man as a part of mankind, or as a human being, as in "Man is a weak creature." Some languages make no distinction between "come" and "go" (both contain the idea of motion, but "come" implies that the motion is toward the speaker, "go" that it is away from the speaker). English has no word that includes both brothers and sisters, as "parents" includes both father and mother; other languages have a single word that takes in both, like German *Geschwister*.

The arrangement of words into sentences is very important in some languages, less so in others. In English, "Peter sees Paul" tells us that Peter does the seeing, while Paul is seen; but the only thing that tells us is that Peter comes at the beginning, while Paul follows "sees." In Latin, we could put Paul first and Peter last, and still have the sentence mean "Peter sees Paul," because the doer of the action would have a *-us* ending, the receiver of the action a *-um* ending *(Paulum videt Petrus)*. Latin in this case would use little bits of machinery, or endings, that English also once used, but later gave up in favor of the arrangement of words that puts the doer first and the receiver last.

So we see that while the basic machinery of language is the same (sounds, words, sentences) there is infinite variation in the choice of sounds, the exact meaning of words, the arrangement of sentences, the use or non-use of endings. Each language is a law unto itself.

In spite of all these differences, there is a sort of basic unity in all spoken languages. This unity comes in part from the fact that they all use the same basic machinery, but even more from the fact that they all have a single purpose. The purpose is to convey and transfer thought from one human brain to another, to make understanding possible between two or more human beings. Understanding is what leads to our working together, to our carrying on any kind of group activity, to civilization. All this would be impossible without the transfer of meanings, thoughts and ideas from one brain to another.

Words only stand for thoughts. They are not the thoughts themselves. This is proved by the fact that different languages have different words for the same thing. Words are symbols of thoughts.

We must not let symbols dazzle us to the point where we think they are the objects they stand for. It is not enough to say or write "bread" or "freedom," if neither the bread nor the freedom is there. We must recognize and use symbols for what they are, and make ourselves their masters, not their slaves.

Above all, we must strive to make our word-symbols clear, so that they will hold pretty much the same meaning for the one who produces them and the one who receives them. Otherwise, there will be confusion and lack of understanding—the same sort of thing that is described in the story of the Tower of Babel.

Language, the set of symbols by which we transfer thoughts and meanings, is important. We must watch it and study it. We must try to perfect it. Its machinery is important, too—its sounds, words and sentences. We cannot afford to be sloppy or careless about them, any more than we would be sloppy or careless about the car we drive or the bicycle we ride. We don't want them to break down when we most need them. Neither do we want language to break down when we most need it. Machinery needs oil, repairs, attention. So does language.

PART TWO

HOW DOES LANGUAGE WORK?

1 *Language Helps Everybody*

IF ONE WERE TO TAKE THE TROUBLE TO count up all the words in the dictionaries, he would reach a total running into six figures—the hundreds of thousands. There is no single dictionary that holds all the words in use, though some library dictionaries, in several volumes, come fairly close. It has been figured that all the words in the English language are somewhere around the million mark. About the same total holds for other great civilized languages, like French, German or Spanish.

No speaker of a language knows all of that language's words. In fact, the average speaker is lucky if he knows one-tenth of them.

What about all the words you or I don't know, and have probably never seen or heard—about nine out of ten in the big dictionaries?

Some of them are words that we shall get to learn sooner or later, because we keep on learning throughout our lives. Some are words that used to be familiar and popular back in the days of Chaucer, or Shakespeare, or even Dickens, but that now are no longer used. Others are slang words, or words used in only one part of the English-speaking world and not in others.

But the majority are words used in special fields of human endeavor, and unfamiliar to people outside those fields. We might call them technical words, save for the fact that "technical" brings to mind something linked with science and mechanics. Actually, every field of activity has its own special set of technical words and expressions, which people who do not work in that field often barely recognize, or do not recognize at all. Such words form group languages, which serve special groups.

Take, for instance, religion. If you attend one church, you may be familiar with the exact meaning of "cassock" and "surplice." If you attend another, you may know all about "shofar" and "Torah." Many religious words and expressions are known to everyone: "angel," "hymn," "psalm" and the like. Religion is served by language and in turn contributes to language words and terms.

Some of our words of religion are Hebrew or Aramaic (Aramaic was a language closely resembling Hebrew, and was spoken by the Jews at the time of Christ). "Abbot," for instance, is the Aramaic *abba*, meaning "father," while "cherub" and "seraph," with their strange plural forms "cherubim" and "seraphim," are Hebrew. Many more religious words come from Greek, the language in which the New Testament was first recorded. "Priest," for example, is the Greek *presbyter*, or "elder," a word from which we also get "Presbyterian." "Bishop" is the English form taken by Greek *episcopos*, or "overseer." "Monk" is Greek *monachos*, one who leads a lonely life. Then there are Latin words, like "altar" and "Communion"; French words, like "prayer" and "chapel," native Anglo-Saxon words, like "holy" and "gospel." Some of our religious words have stories connected with them. "Gospel," for instance, is "God's spell," or the Word of God. The original meaning of "chapel" is "little cape" or "little cloak"; the first chapel was built to mark the spot where Saint Martin, a soldier in the Roman army, donated half of his military cape to a freezing beggar, who turned out to be Christ. You would hardly think of "good-bye" as a religious expression, yet its early form was "God be with you."

If you go in for business and finance, you will find that you will have to become acquainted with many special words and their exact meaning: "credit" and "debit," "inflation" and "deduction," "equity" and "recapitalization." You will find that certain common expressions come straight from the business world. You may find yourself in debt, and say that you are "in the red." Why? Because it is the practice of business firms in keeping their books to enter their profits, gains or credits in black ink, but their losses or debits in red ink. In stock trading on Wall Street you will hear of "bull markets," "bears," "lambs," "wildcat issues," "stop-loss orders" and "out the window."

Business and trade depend almost entirely on language, particularly in the matter of advertising. The product must be made attractive to the prospective buyer, and this is accomplished mainly by written and spoken words. It is not enough to offer for sale a steak, a drink or a toothpaste. The steak must be described as "sizzling," "juicy," "tender," the beverage as "sparkling," "cooling," "refreshing," the toothpaste as "sanitary," "hygienic," "health-giving."

There is, of course, the danger that in some forms of advertising what is being sold is words rather than products, that you are actually buying the sizzle rather than the steak. This is something one must learn to watch against.

If one goes into the field of law and government, one runs up against a very large and very special class of words and expressions which are apt to bewilder those who don't know them. Legal terminology makes abundant use of French and Latin words, and the surprising thing about them is that a good many have gotten out into everyday speech. Take the word "posse," that appears in so many

Western stories. This is originally a Latin word meaning "to be able"; it also happens to be the opening word in an old legal formula, all in Latin, which was used in giving a marshal or sheriff authority "to be able" to gather a certain number of citizens to help him catch criminals. Words like "alias" and "alibi," much used in mystery stories, are likewise Latin and taken from the language of the law. The first means "otherwise," "otherwise called," and the second means "elsewhere." From French legal language brought into English by the Normans come such popular words as "jury" and "dime." The former goes back to a word that means "to swear an oath" (juries are sworn in), while "dime" means in origin "tenth," and used to refer to that fraction of one's income which it was customary in the Middle Ages to contribute to the support of the church; we use it in the more recent sense of "one-tenth of a dollar."

Politics and government are great coiners, as well as great users, of words, expressions and style. Political terms coined in the past, but still much in use today, include "log-rolling" and "filibuster," "Gerrymander" and "Tory." Of late, government bureaus have been accused of creating a form of language which no one, including the creators themselves, can understand, and to this the name "Gobbledegook" has been applied (the name is supposed to imitate the gobbling of a turkey, which is noisy but meaningless). Gobbledegook includes such rare words as "disincentive" and "dichotomy," and phrases like "unexpended portion of the day's rations."

When we come to the field of science and technology we find that we are really lost in a tangle of terms the precise meaning of which is known only to the specialists in each individual branch. Medical terms, including the names of bodily organs and diseases, drugs and medicines, surgical instruments and appliances, run into the hundreds of thousands, and are for the most part taken from Latin or Greek. Then we have all the terms used by the physicists, the chemists, the biologists, the astronomers, the geologists, the meteorologists, the engineers. They are clear and precise to those who coin them and use them, but not to the rest of us. When an atomic scientist speaks of a "thermonuclear reaction," an anthropologist of an "artifact," a biologist of a "chromosome," a surgeon of "hemostasia," it is hard to follow them, unless we have gone into that field. Yet many scientific words have gotten into our everyday speech, often in shortened form, like "sulfa" and "mike" for "sulfanilamide" and "microphone." It is safe to say that fully half of the million or so words that go into our largest dictionaries are scientific in nature.

There is a set of words, or type of language, that serves each individual industry or occupation. Railroad men have a jargon of their own; they use, for instance, "fish" for "passengers," "tallow-pot" for "fireman," "snake" for "switchman." Hotel bellboys refer to a tip as a "Higgins" and a non-tipper as a "stiff." Cowboys have their own special language, which often breaks out into the movies or on TV, and with portions of which you are acquainted. There is a vocabulary of flying, one of jet propulsion, which occasionally gets into space travel stories, one of military ordnance. There is one of farming and one of flower-raising. There is a special set of words used by those who collect stamps, and another by those who collect coins (these two hobbies, by the way, go by the names of "philately" and "numismatics").

Then there is the vast vocabulary of sports, which spills over into everyday life to a degree that few of us suspect, but which also has secret and mysterious angles known only to the devotees of each individual sport or game.

America's most typically national sport, baseball, is now becoming widely popular throughout the world, and its terms are being readily translated into Japanese, French, Spanish, Italian and other languages. Yet think how bewildering they are to one who does not know the game! A word like "strike," which in labor relations means a work stoppage, is used in baseball to indicate either a pitch coming within an area where the batter could reasonably hit it, or an unsuccessful attempt on the batter's part to connect with such a pitch. "Ball" normally means the round sphere itself; but that is not what the umpire means when he tells the batter to take his base on four balls. The same thing applies to "pitch," "catch," "field," "base," "foul," all words which are used with much different meanings outside the diamond (which, by the way, is another word that has a very special baseball meaning).

On the other hand, there are all sorts of expressions that started in baseball and worked their way into many everyday situations: "to play ball with someone," "to pinch-hit for someone," "to put it across" ("the plate" is understood). What goes for baseball goes for other sports, like football, boxing, running, and for games like bridge, chess and poker. On the one hand you have terms like "end run," "forward pass," "to place," "to show," "rook," "full house," which belong to the vocabulary of the individual game and would carry little or no meaning to the person unacquainted with it; but on the other, you have terms like "sidestep," "trump," "checkmate," "poker-face," "neck and neck," "stymied," that have gotten into general use in the language.

Language enters all human activities and few, if any, of them could be carried on without language. Language describes them, limits them, accompanies them at every step, makes them possible. Language literally helps everybody. It normally starts with the family, which first teaches language to its younger members, then goes on to the church, the school, the community, the government, the world of business and industry, the world of amusement and entertainment, the world of science. Each part of society, each occupation and trade has its own peculiar, limited language, but all are joined together by the common stock of words and expressions, the one word out of ten that they all share. Words like "hepatitis," "pi" and "gasket" may belong to only a small part of the population, but words like "and," "the," "come," "go," "bread," "water," "good," "bad" belong to all of us.

Therefore, we should not worry if we do not know all the words in the language. Nobody does. What we should do is to make sure we know those words that everybody uses, know what they mean and how to use them. Then we can go ahead and expand our vocabulary, learn more words, their meanings and uses. The more we learn, the more power we have. The better we use our language, the more friends we shall make. People like those who share their own knowledge and experiences. The more we can talk to people in their own language, and with their own words, the more they will like us.

2 *How Language Grows*

WORDS ARE LIKE HUMAN BEINGS. THEY ARE born, they live, they work, they die. If you run your eye over the dictionary pages, you will occasionally come across words that are either marked with a cross or labeled *arch.* or *obs.* (abbreviations for "archaic," which means "old," "antiquated," and "obsolete," which is "out of use"). If you read a play by Shakespeare, you will meet words that you have to look up in the glossary at the end of the book; yet those words were in full use and understood by everybody at the time they were written.

Here are a couple of sentences that could conceivably have been written or spoken in Shakespeare's days: "Daw, you have begecked me! I yuke to pingle with you and yerk you until you ghost!" Would you like a twentieth-century translation? Here it is: "Fool, you have cheated me! I itch to fight with you and hit you until you die!" What has really died is a whole set of words in the statements.

But to compensate us for the words that have died since Shakespeare's time, how many have been born! What would Shakespeare have made of this? "Your play will be broadcast and televised over this network by a coast-to-coast hookup!"

For every word that has become archaic or obsolete, dozens have sprung up. Some are old words simply put together to carry a new meaning. The prefix *tele-* comes from ancient Greek, and means "distance." "Vision" comes to us from Latin through French, and refers to "seeing." Both words would have been understood in Shakespeare's day, but since "seeing at a distance" was not an accepted practice, the complete modern word "television" or "televise" would probably have been associated with witchcraft.

Then there are words about whose origin nobody is quite sure. All we know is that at a certain period of history they began to be used. Two very common words of this type are "boy" and "girl."

Other words come from abroad. If we were to tie ourselves down to only those words that the Anglo-Saxons used, our vocabulary would be poor indeed. But from the very start the speakers of English began to borrow words from their neighbors. They took "church" and "box" from Greek, "cheese" and "street" from Latin, "knife" and "leg" from the language of the Danes who mingled with them on English soil. Later, when the Normans came into England with William the Conqueror, they brought with them hundreds of French words that merged into the language and gave rise to such common, everyday words as "pay" and "very." Still later, writers brought into the English language more Latin and Greek words which they thought would add to the expressiveness of the language, words like "education" and "apostrophe." All the way through its history, English has taken words from other tongues. Today we have "piano" and "studio" from Italian, "mosquito" and "stampede" from Spanish, "yacht" and "freight" from Dutch, "halt" and "poodle" from German, "syrup" and "sofa" from Arabic, "candy" and "check" from Persian, "tomahawk" and "chocolate" from the languages of the American Indians.

Some words are intentionally built to resemble other

words already in use. "Cavalcade" and "panorama" are old words, but "motorcade" and "cinerama" are quite recent. Those who thought them up figured that words ending in *-ade* or *-cade* would give the idea of objects or people filing past in a procession ("parade," too, may have helped in creating this notion), while *-rama* would convey the general impression of a big display; actually, the ending should be not *-rama*, but *-orama*, since it comes from Greek *orao*, "I see," and "cinerama" should really be spelt "cinorama."

There are many words in English which are used in several different ways. "Run" in "run to second base" does not have the same meaning as "run in a stocking." A "box of candy" and "to box in the ring" show different meanings. In most of these cases, the word started out with one meaning, then gradually added the others. A "diamond," for instance, is in origin a precious stone; but since a baseball diamond is shaped somewhat like the cut stone, the name was applied to it. The boxing "ring" was at first any kind of a round arena for games and sports, shaped like the "ring" on your finger; and even today, when boxing rings are square, the name continues to be used. This increase in the number of uses doesn't really add to the number of words, but it does add to the number of meanings, and dictionaries often make separate entries for the same word used in separate ways.

Changes in meaning sometimes involve the disappearance of the older usage, and the survival only of the new. The word "foyer" comes to us from French, in which language it originally meant "fireplace." This was its first meaning in English too; then it came to be applied to a large room where there was a fireplace, like the lobby of a hotel or theater, or the large entrance hall of a house or an apartment. Today, few foyers have fireplaces, but the name lives on in its new sense.

Sometimes meanings are completely changed. "Silly" was once "blessed" (it comes from the same source as "soul"). Then it became "one so good as to be foolish," a "blessed fool"; finally the "blessed" idea wore away, and only the "foolish" idea was left. "Nice," on the other hand, comes from a Latin-French word that means "foolish." When medieval philosophers wrangled, they often made "nice" (that is, "foolish," "trifling," "hair-splitting") distinctions. These "nice" distinctions came to be admired at times for their subtlety. Finally "nice" became "pleasing," and that is the way it is used today.

Occasionally a word that is used by two or more different languages changes its meaning in one but not in the other. When this happens, it leads to confusion as you go from one language to the other. You hear *rente* in French, and you imagine it is the same word as "rent" in English. So it is, and English got it from French; but in French it means "income." English got it at a time when practically the only form of income one could have was from rent on lands or buildings. English kept it that way, while French went on to give it the additional meaning of "income" from any source. English "knight" and German *Knecht* are similarly related. The German word means "serf," which at first glance seems far removed from "knight." But a knight had a subordinate position in the medieval world, being bound to serve either the king or a higher nobleman.

These differences in meaning may, and often do appear in the same language as spoken in different parts of the world. To an American speaker of English, "corn" means that vegetable which you eat off the cob. To the Britisher, it means cereal "grain" in general, and particularly wheat, and this is the original meaning of "corn." How did the Americans get their meaning? Our American corn was not known until the discovery of the New World, and when the first settlers found the Indians using it, they called it either by its native name, "maize," or by the name of "Indian corn." Their descendants, however, gradually left out the "Indian," and since they had other words, like "wheat" and "grain," for what they had originally called "corn," they finally applied "corn" to the Indian variety only.

The study of word-meanings is called semantics, from a Greek word *semaino*, "I mean." Every time you look up the exact meaning of a word in a dictionary, you are doing research in semantics. The term semantics also applies to the examination of changes in the meanings of words deliberately attempted by some person or group for their own special purposes. Some words are used as slogans, surrounded by other carefully picked words, and finally given special meanings. A word like "people," for instance, is something you have heard and used all your life. It is a harmless word when you speak of "the people in this room" or "the people of the United States of America." It is a word that you rather like, and that brings a feeling of warm, pleasant companionship to your mind. Knowing this, the Communists have taken over the word and applied it to their own political activities. They speak of "people's republic," "people's court," "people's army" when, as a matter of fact, the people of their countries have very little to do with running these activities. They hope that by the use of a word you like you will acquire the feeling that Communist institutions are, like ours, run by and for the people, which they are not. This misuse of common, familiar words is something one must guard against.

The language processes we have been describing apply not only to English, but to all languages. In all of them you will find words dying out and words being born, words being created out of thin air and old words being put together to form new words, words being taken from other languages and words changing their uses and their meanings. The feature of constant change is common to all languages. The only thing that varies is the rate and speed of change.

People sometimes speak of Latin and Greek as "dead" languages. Nothing could be farther from the truth. Latin continued to be spoken long after the fall of Rome. It was the language used by scholars in all the nations of western Europe during the Middle Ages and the Renaissance. It continues to be spoken today by priests in the Roman Catholic Church, and is brought periodically up to date by the coinage of such expressions as *birota ignifero latice incita* ("two-wheeled conveyance driven by a fire-bearing juice") for the modern motorcycle, which the Romans, of course, did not have.

It may also be said that Latin lives on in its direct descendants, the Romance languages, French, Spanish, Italian, Portuguese, Rumanian, any one of which is a straight continuation, with changes but without a break, of the tongue used by the Romans. Lastly, Latin lives on in the many words, scientific and otherwise, which we use daily. When you use "extra," "super," "bonus," "item," "propaganda," "veto," "video," you are using pure, unchanged Latin.

As for Greek, it never died in any sense of the word. From the time of the ancient Greeks, it continued to be spoken in the Roman Empire of the East, whose capital was Constantinople, or Byzantium, and is still the popular spoken language of Greece today. In addition, it has contributed a very large part of our scientific and technical vocabulary, and there is practically no hour of the day when you don't use a Greek word ("phone," "gym," "electric," "arithmetic," "geography" are a few of them).

What is true of Latin and Greek is, of course, even more true of the modern foreign languages. In French, Spanish, German, Italian and all the others you will find changes going on that are very similar to our own.

Language reflects the activities of the human beings who speak it. These activities are forever changing, evolving, turning into something new. Don't be astonished, then, to find language likewise passing from one form to another. Don't think of language today as being the last and final form that language will take. If you could come back to life two hundred years from now, you would find not only the world and its activities transformed, but also its languages. Among them would be an English language that you would be able to recognize and understand in part, but many of whose words and expressions would be completely strange and mysterious to you until they were explained, just as "television" would be strange to Shakespeare if he were to come back to life today.

3 Languages Come in Families

LONG AGO IT WAS SUPPOSED THAT ALL LAN-
guages came from one, and that one was believed to be the
ancient Hebrew of the Old Testament. But in recent centuries, as a result of the discovery of many strange languages spoken in parts of the world which had been
unknown during the Middle Ages, the opposite view began
to prevail—that all of the earth's languages could not in any
way have come down from a single original tongue. Today, as more facts come to light, people are not so sure,
and the entire question is open.

There are spoken in the world today 2,796 different
languages. Many of them are broken up into separate dialects, and at times the dialects of a single language are so
different that the people speaking the various dialects barely
manage to understand one another. You may have noticed
that if you go to see a movie produced in Britain with
British actors, some of the words they speak occasionally
sound strange. Americans and Britishers both speak English, but the two ways of speaking are dialects of the same
language. You may also notice differences in speech between a man who comes from New England, one who
comes from the South, and one who comes from the Midwest. Their different ways of speaking are also dialects of
the same language. There are languages where the dialect
differences are much more noticeable than they are in
English.

English, with all its dialects, comes closer to some foreign languages than it does to others. If an American says "bread," a German says *Brot*, and a Norwegian says *brod*, it is fairly obvious that the three languages are somehow related. This relationship does not hinge on their having borrowed words from one another (though this has taken place, too) because words in which similarity appears are words that have been in all these languages as far back as we can trace them. Besides, they show similarity in the way they put words and sentences together, and these similarities become greater the farther back we go. So we feel justified in putting languages that show this close relationship into one family, which we call Germanic because when it first appeared in history it was located mainly in what is today Germany. Germanic languages are English, German and Dutch, as well as the four Scandinavian tongues (Swedish, Norwegian, Danish and Icelandic). Notice how close these languages are: English says "good morning"; German has *"guten Morgen"*; Dutch has *"goeden morgen"*; Swedish *"god morgon"*; Norwegian and Danish *"god morgen."*

Now we go to another group of languages that show the same striking resemblances among themselves, along with a more distant resemblance to the Germanic group. The Romance languages are so called because they come from Latin, the language of the Romans. Speakers of Romance and speakers of Germanic have been in close touch throughout their histories, and they have borrowed heavily from each other. English, in particular, has taken over a very large number of words from French, as well as from the Latin that the Romance languages came from. But in addition, Germanic and Romance show certain original resemblances that were not borrowed, both in words and in the way words and sentences are put together. A word like "video" was taken only a few years ago by English from Latin, where it means "I see." In Italian, which comes directly from Latin, "I see" is *vedo;* in Spanish it's *veo;* so we can see that Latin, Italian and Spanish are very closely linked. In English, we use an entirely different word, "see."

But in English we also have a native word, not borrowed at any time from Latin, which nevertheless shows an original kinship to the Latin word. That word is "wit." Now "wit" has to do with knowledge, not with sight. But isn't seeing one of the best ways of gaining knowledge? In Greek, another branch of the bigger family, a word resembling "wit" and *video* means "hear." Hearing is another way of knowing. This is what apparently happened: the speakers of the original language from which Germanic, Latin and Greek all came had a word which could carry all three meanings: "see," "hear" and "know." As they spread apart and subdivided themselves into separate groups, all retained the word, though each made changes in it; but each group fastened on a single meaning. The ancient inhabitants of northern India called their sacred books the Vedas, which meant "knowledge." So they belonged to the big family, too. Their word comes closer to the Latin in appearance, but closer to the English in meaning. The Russian word for "see" is *vidyet'*, and this shows that Russian, too, is a member of the family.

What shall we call this big family of languages that runs from northern India all the way across Europe? Various names have been given to it, but the one most commonly used is "Indo-European," a name that seems to cover the geographical picture.

This Indo-European family of languages has eight

branches that are still alive today: the Germanic, which we have described, and which includes English; the Latin-Romance, which we have also described; the Greek; the Slavic (here we find Russian, Polish, Czech, and the languages of Yugoslavia); the Albanian and the Armenian (both very small); the Celtic (Irish and Welsh are both Celtic tongues); and the Indo-Iranian, which covers northern and central India, Pakistan, Iran and Afghanistan, and of which the best known modern members are Hindustani and Persian.

But this does not by any means exhaust the list of all the earth's languages, though it does include just about half of all the earth's inhabitants. There are many other families of languages, some large, some small. Within each family you have the same sort of relationship that exists among the Indo-European languages. But when you try to link these other families either to Indo-European or to one another, you have a very hard time.

Take another important family of languages, the Semitic. Here you have, to mention only two, Hebrew and Arabic. You have no trouble at all proving that Hebrew and Arabic are as close to each other as are English and German. But when you try to establish a link between them and Latin, you find that it doesn't work out.

Some of these language families that don't seem to connect with Indo-European are very large. One of them includes Chinese, which is the largest single language in the world, along with languages spoken in Siam (or Thailand, if you prefer the new name), Burma and Tibet. Another includes Finnish and Hungarian and, possibly, Turkish. Still another covers Japanese and, maybe, Korean. Then there is the big Malayo-Polynesian family, which appears mainly in the islands of the Indian and Pacific Oceans, run-

INDO-EUROPEAN
HAMITO-SEMITIC
URAL-ALTAIC
SINO-TIBETAN
JAPANESE-KOREAN
DRAVIDIAN
MALAYO-POLYNESIAN
SUDANESE-GUINEAN

HOTTENTOT-BUSHMAN
AUSTRALIAN AND PAPUAN
AM. INDIAN AND ESKIMO

MUNDA-MON-KHMER
BASQUE
HYPERBOREAN
BANTU
CAUCASIAN
AINU

ning from Madagascar off the east coast of Africa to Easter Island, off the west coast of South America, and taking in the native languages of Malaya, Indonesia, New Zealand, the Philippines and Hawaii. Dravidian is the name applied to a family of languages spoken in southern India.

In North, Central and South America you find over one thousand American Indian languages, most of them small, but a few still widely spoken, especially in countries like Mexico, Peru, Bolivia and Paraguay. These American Indian languages have been grouped into families, but it is as hard to prove kinship among these families as between Indo-European and Semitic. Something similar happens in Africa, where you have hundreds of languages spoken by the African Negroes, and in Australia, where there are at least a hundred native languages.

The total of 2,796 languages in existence today is very unevenly distributed, both among language families and for what concerns the number of people who speak them. If each language had the same number of speakers, there would be about one million speakers for each tongue. But most of the American Indian, African and Australian languages have far fewer; some have only a few hundred people speaking them.

At the other end of the line stand the language giants—languages with over fifty million speakers. They are easy to tell about, because there are only thirteen of them. First in numbers comes Chinese, with about 450 million speakers and numerous dialects. Next is English, which has over 250 million speakers in the United States and possessions, the British Isles, British Dominions like Canada, Australia, New Zealand and South Africa, and British possessions scattered all over the globe. The third biggest language is one you would hardly guess—Hindustani, spoken in India and Pakis-

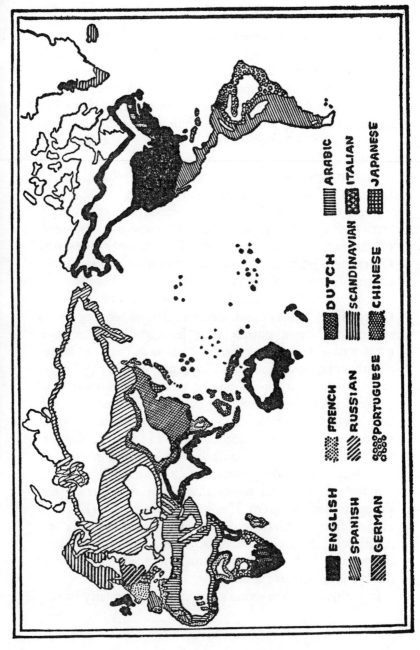

ENGLISH FRENCH DUTCH ARABIC

SPANISH RUSSIAN SCANDINAVIAN ITALIAN

GERMAN PORTUGUESE CHINESE JAPANESE

tan by close to 200 million people. Russian, Spanish and German all hover around the 100 million mark, though Russian may lay claim to 150 million if we include two very closely related tongues spoken in the Soviet Union, Ukrainian and Bielorussian, or White Russian. Somewhere between 70 and 100 million are French and Japanese. Then, between 50 and 70 million, we have Italian; the Malay of Indonesia; the Bengali of northeastern India; Portuguese, spoken in Brazil as well as in Portugal; and Arabic, the main language of North Africa and the Near East.

Some of these languages cover tremendous expanses of territory. English, for instance, holds sway over one-fifth of the earth's land surface, and Russian over one-sixth. Others, like Japanese and Italian, are restricted to small territories. Some are widely scattered, like English and French, which have footholds in every corner of the earth. Others, like Chinese, Hindustani and Bengali, are not much spoken or known outside their homelands. Some have greater advantages than others as carriers of trade, or scientific thought, or art, music and literature. We in the United States, basing our choice on the contributions these languages have made to our own culture, have concentrated largely on French, Spanish, German and Italian, along with the two great Classical tongues, Latin and Greek. But we may have to change our point of view and give greater attention to some of the others, notably Russian, Chinese and Hindustani. You will notice that six of the thirteen are European and Western Hemisphere languages (English, French, Spanish, German, Italian and Portuguese); six are Asiatic and African (Chinese, Japanese, Hindustani, Malay, Bengali and Arabic); and one, Russian, spreads over eastern Europe and northern Asia.

English, among the world's languages, is singularly fortunate. It has the second largest speaking population, widely scattered all over the earth. It is the recognized language of business and trade exchanges, and its speakers possess over half of the world's economic wealth and means of communication—railroads, automobiles, telephones, radio stations, newspapers, motion pictures. It is one of the greatest scientific languages, and nearly half of the world's scientific reports are written in English. It has a long and beautiful literature. It is small wonder that many people, both here and abroad, when they think of a single language to serve the entire world, think of English.

Yet we must not forget the claims of other languages in this matter—languages like French, which long served as the cultural and diplomatic tongue of Europe, or Spanish, the leading tongue of the Western Hemisphere south of the Rio Grande, or German, the main language of central Europe, or Chinese and Hindustani and Russian, with their tremendous masses of speakers and ancient and modern cultures. Perhaps a compromise language is needed to reconcile the conflicting claims of all these great world languages.

Meanwhile, we must think of them all, as well as of the rest of the 2,796. We must respect them all, because each one of them means as much to its own speakers as English means to us.

4 Places and People

WHY ARE PLACES CALLED BY CERTAIN names? The names, of course, were all bestowed by people who at one time or another lived there. Sometimes old names are kept, sometimes new ones are given.

Take New York, for instance. The first Dutch settlers knew it as New Amsterdam, after the city of Amsterdam in Holland. Before them, the Indians had the name of Manhattan for the island which today is only one of the city's five boroughs. There is a story that Manhattan, in the language of the Delaware Indians whom the Dutch found, means "the place where we got drunk," and that they created the name after Henry Hudson had made them a present of a barrel of rum, but this is by no means certain.

At all events, when the English took the city from the Dutch, they rechristened it New York, after the ancient town of York in England. But York was not the original name of the English town. It was the way the Anglo-Saxons pronounced Eboracum, the older name used by the Romans and the British Celts. As to what Eboracum meant in the first place, there is a lot of doubt, so that in the end the origin of "New York" becomes just as obscure as that of "Manhattan."

Many of our States have Indian names, like Oklahoma, Tennessee and Kentucky. Others were named after English and French kings and queens, like Louisiana, Georgia, North and South Carolina and Virginia. Then we have some that remind us of famous men (Delaware, Washington, Pennsylvania), and others that are named after European or even American regions (New Jersey, New Hampshire, Maine, Rhode Island, New Mexico). Florida, Nevada and Montana are Spanish names, bestowed by their earliest settlers or explorers ("Flowery," "Snowy" and "Mountain" would be the English equivalents). Vermont is French, and means Green Mountain.

What goes for States goes for cities, counties, mountains, rivers. Chicago is an Indian name, meaning "place of skunk smells," because wild onions grew on the spot; but St. Louis is French, after King Louis IX of France, whom the Catholic Church proclaimed a saint after his death. Bismarck, the capital of North Dakota, is named after the Iron Chancellor of Prussia, who brought about German unification in 1870, while Columbus, Ohio, commemorates America's discoverer. Rome, N.Y., and Rome, Ga., are named after the great city of ancient times which is now Italy's capital. Other names taken from ancient cities are Utica, Ithaca, Troy, Syracuse, Athens. Alleghanies is an Indian name, but Rocky Mountains and Sierra Nevada are descriptive (the latter is Spanish, and means "Snowy Range"). Mississippi is Indian ("Father of Waters"), while the Hudson and Delaware rivers are named after men.

Place-names in other parts of the world have stories to tell, too, if we can only decipher them. But to do that, we have to learn a few words in strange tongues. What is the Rio Grande? It's the "Big River" in Spanish, which is the language spoken by the inhabitants of Mexico and most of Central and South America, outside of Brazil, which is Portuguese-speaking. However, notice that Rio is "river," and Grande is "big." Spanish, and the Romance languages generally, usually put the adjective after the noun, not before, as we do. Now if you come across Rio Seco in your reading of Western stories, and I tell you that Seco means "dry," you'll know what the name means. You already know that Sierra is "mountain range." Can you figure out Sierra Madre?

Latin America is a term that embraces both Spanish- and Portuguese-speaking lands to the south of us. It can even cover Haiti, which speaks French, since Spanish, Portuguese and French all come from Latin. Place-names in Latin America are just like our own. Many come from the languages of the local American Indians: this is true of countries like Mexico, Peru, Uruguay, Paraguay, cities like Taxco in Mexico, Lima and Cuzco in Peru, Quito in Ecuador, rivers like the Paraná, mountains like the Andes. Then there is a whole series named after places in Spain, from which came most of the settlers to Latin-American lands—Guadalajara in Mexico, Córdoba in Argentina, Santiago in Chile. Others are named after the great men of Latin America; Bolivia, for example, is named after Simón Bolívar, a man who played in South America much the same role that George Washington played for us. His chief aide's name was Sucre, and one of the important cities of Bolivia is named after him. Other names are descriptive and easily translated.

Argentina is "Silvery," and the Rio de la Plata means "River of Silver." Argentina's capital, Buenos Aires, means "good airs" or "fair winds." Brazil's capital, Rio de Janeiro, means "River of January," because in that month it was discovered; this is Portuguese, not Spanish, but the two languages are close; if Spanish explorers instead of Portuguese had discovered it, they would have called it Río de Enero. Colombia is named after Columbus, just like our own Columbia. Venezuela is "Little Venice." Why? Venice, as you know, is built on canals; the first explorers who came to Venezuela found the natives living in villages built on stilts right out on the water, and this reminded them of old-world Venice. Two other interesting place-names are Yucatán in Mexico and Patagonia in the extreme south of Argentina. In the first, the natives called out "Yucatán!" at the Spanish explorers, who thought they were being given .the name of the land; only later they found out that it meant "What do you say?" In Patagonia, the explorers found giant footsteps in the sand of the beach where they landed. "Big Foot" in Spanish is *patacón*, and they named the country Patagonia, or "land of the big feet."

Old-World place-names are just as fascinating. England is the land of the Angles, who along with the Saxons and Jutes invaded the country in the Fifth Century A.D., but Britain is the land of the Britons, the earlier Celtic inhabitants, who retreated into Wales and became the Welsh. This name, however, was given them by their Anglo-Saxon foes, and means "foreigner," "stranger." The name the Welsh give themselves is Cymry, and it appears in Cumberland. The Saxons seem to have gotten their name from a dagger they used in fighting, called *seaxna*. The name of Scotland was at one time applied to Ireland, which the Romans called Scotia Major, or "greater Scotland." Towns and rivers in the British Isles are sometimes Anglo-Saxon, sometimes Danish, sometimes Norman-French, but more often Latin or Celtic. We have already seen how Eboracum turned to York. In the same way the Celtic-Roman Londinium became London, and the river Tamisius became the Thames. The Romans called their fortified encampments, around which cities grew up, *castrum*, and this word, used as an ending, turned into English *-cester*,

-chester and *-caster* in names like Worcester, Manchester, Lancaster, most of which crossed the ocean and are used in America as well.

On the European continent, we find such names as France, Germany, Paris, Berlin, Seine, Alps, Mediterranean. France is named after the Franks, a Germanic tribe which in the fifth century overran the old Roman province of Gaul. The name "frank" meant "free," "free-born," and we still find it today used in that meaning, especially in connection with stamps. The older name of the country, Gaul, seems to be connected with the Latin *gallus*, "rooster," and a crowing rooster is still the symbol of France. Germany, on the other hand, is connected with the Latin *germanus*, "kindred." The German name for the country is Deutschland, or "People's Land." If we travel in Europe or collect stamps we will find many countries whose names for themselves are quite different from ours. Hungary, for instance, is Magyarország to the Hungarians, Finland is Suomi to the Finns, and Greece is Hellas to the Greeks.

Paris gets its name from an ancient Gaulish tribe, the Parisii, whom the Romans found in that spot when they came to Gaul around 50 B.C. Berlin, the capital of Germany, has a Slavic name, and means "Wasteland," indicating that only marshes were there before the city was built.

The Seine River, on which Paris is built, is named after another ancient Gaulish tribe, the Sequani. The Alps may have a name connected with *albus*, Latin for "white," but we are not quite sure. The Mediterranean means "between lands," and if you look at the map you will see the reason: Europe is on one side, Africa on the other. The Romans used to call it Mare Internum, or "Inland Sea."

Of special interest to us are the place-names of Spain, because so many of them have been transplanted to our own southwest. Spanish rivers and cities often start with *Guadal-*, which is Arabic for "river the" or "river of the." Guadalquivir, for instance, is Wad al Kibir, "river the big." They might as well have called it Rio Grande. Why did they use an Arabic name instead of a Spanish one? Because the Arabic-speaking Moors from North Africa overran Spain in the Eighth Century A.D., and stayed there until 1492, the year America was discovered.

Toledo, Ohio, is named after Toledo in Spain. The original Sierra Nevada is in Spain, too. All our place-names beginning with San or Santa are Spanish (San Francisco, San José, Santa Barbara), and most of them started in Spain, which is a land of great religious devotion to the Saints.

Russian place-names sound strange, but they become very simple once they are translated. The ending *-grad* or *-gorod* means "town," so that Stalingrad is Stalintown, and Novgorod is Newtown. Similar endings appear in other countries using Slavic languages. Belgrade, the capital of Yugoslavia, is "White Town."

In Asia, we find many lands whose name ends in *-stan* (Hindustan, Pakistan, Afghanistan). This is just a Persian word meaning "land." Many cities of India end in *-abad* or *-pur*, which mean "town." Allahabad, for instance, is "God's city." China to the Chinese is Chung Kuo, or "Middle Land." Names of Chinese rivers often end in Ho, which means "river." So don't say Hoang Ho River, or you'll be saying "Yellow River River." The *-king* in Peking and Nanking means "capital," the first being the North Capital, the second the South Capital.

Names of places make you curious about names of

people. Does everybody have a name? How did the custom of giving names get started? In primitive tribes, people often have the same names that are given animals: "Growler," "Biter," "Grumbler," "Lightfoot." Animal names like "bear" and "wolf" were originally of this type; "bear," in many Indo-European languages appears as either "brown" or "bruiser." These names were applied to people without change, perhaps in the hope that they would acquire the better qualities of the animal involved. Accordingly, in Latin you have names like Ursus, "bear," Leo, "lion," Lupus, "wolf"; Leo and Ursula ("little she-bear") are still in use today. The Germanic tribes had similar names, often combined with qualities, like Adolph, "noble wolf," and Rudolph, "famous wolf." Other names in which animals are not involved are Vincent ("winning" or "winner" in Latin); Theodore ("God's gift" in Greek); Albert ("honor-bright" in Germanic); Edward ("wealth's guardian" in Anglo-Saxon). Old Hebrew names from the Bible are more religious in nature. The ending -el in Daniel, Samuel, Emanuel, means "God" or "of God." Joseph, Joshua, John, Mary, Miriam are all Hebrew names, and two of them, John and Mary, seem to be the most popular in all western lands, including our own (about twenty million people in the United States are named John or Mary). Mary is easily recognizable in most foreign forms (Marie, Maria, etc.), but John takes strange forms. It's Jean in French, Juan in Spanish, Giovanni in Italian, João in Portuguese, Johannes, cut down to Johann or Hans, in German, Ivan in Russian, Sean in Irish, Juhana in Finnish.

Family names, in the form we know them, got started in the Middle Ages when, as the population increased, it became more and more necessary to distinguish between one John and another. So it got to be John Williamson, or Williams for short, if his father's name was William. Davis is really David's (son). Fitz-, Mac- and Ap- (in Fitzgerald, McHugh, Aprichard or Pritchard) all mean "son of," but Fitz is Norman French, Mc or Mac is Irish or Scots, Ap is Welsh. In many languages, "John son of William," with both names changing each generation, goes on to this day, but the big step in names of this kind was taken when they became fixed and were applied to all descendants, no matter how far removed, so that Williams or Williamson became the regular family name.

Another type of family name is the one that defines the occupation of the family founder—James Baker, or John Taylor. The most popular name of this type, both here and in many foreign lands, is Smith, which takes the form Ferrier in French, Herrero in Spanish, Ferraro in Italian, Schmidt in German, Kusnetsov in Russian. Why is Smith so popular? Because at the time when these family names were formed horseshoeing was very important, and the blacksmith who did it was also the armorer, and made weapons; in fact, he corresponded to the modern automobile mechanic, steel-welder and plumber, all rolled into one.

Next came location names, like Jack London or Leonard Atwell (really "at well"—"at the well"), indicating the place where the founder of the family once lived. Last of all are descriptive names, such as Brown, Long, (or Longfellow), White, Drinkwater, Cruikshanks. The characteristics named have usually long vanished from his descendants, but the name, once given, stuck. You will notice that the descriptive name is often pretty much of a nickname, the only real difference being that the nickname is generally outgrown.

There is another type of nickname which is just an

abbreviation, like Ted or Teddy for Theodore, Ed or Ned for Edward, Tony for Anthony. Sometimes peculiar things happen to abbreviations. Bess for Elizabeth takes into account only the last part of the name, and changes it besides. Jack for John, Peggy for Margaret, are pretty far removed from the original.

In languages other than English we find the same name processes at work, along with others that to us are strange. Corresponding to the -s of our Williams or the -son of Williamson, are -sohn and -sen in German and Scandinavian (Mendelssohn, Jansen). The Romance languages prefer to say "of," which usually comes out as *de* (de Musset, de Avila, de Petri), but since *de* also means "from," it may be like our Atwell rather than our Johnson. Spanish and Portuguese have an ending -ez (Pérez, Gómez) which works like our -s, or -son. Russian has -off or -ov, as well as -sky (Molotoff or Molotov, Vishinsky). The Hungarians and Chinese put the last name first: in Chiang Kai-Shek, Chiang is the family name, while Louis Kossuth, the Hungarian George Washington, is known as Kossuth Lájos in Hungary. Semitic peoples, like the Arabs and Israelis, don't have true family names, but get along with "son of" from generation to generation. David ben Gurion is "David son of Gurion," and David's son Solomon would be known as Solomon ben David. Indonesians specialize in having only one name. The former Indonesian premier was known simply as Soekarno, and that one name was used by all the members of his family.

The ancient Romans had an elaborate series of three names, the first a personal name, the second a family name, the third a nickname that often became attached to the family. Marcus Tullius Cicero, for instance, had Marcus as his first name, Tullius to show that he belonged to the

Tullian clan, and Cicero, meaning "chick-pea" or "wart" because either he or an ancestor had a wart on the nose.

Whether simple or elaborate, all races have names for individuals. They all regard the individual as a unit, worthy of respect and separate identity. Nowhere does the individual merge into the mass to the point of losing his identity or name. Your name is something to be proud of, because it is you.

5 Being Polite at Home and Abroad

POLITENESS IS NOT JUST A SERIES OF EMPTY words; it is a state of mind, showing regard and consideration for the other person's feelings and asking, in return, for the same regard for your own.

Two words got crossed in building up our word "polite." One is the Latin *polio*, "I polish, clean, shine, refine"; the other is the Greek *polis*, meaning "city." This means that politeness is, on the one hand, a clean, polished attitude toward others; on the other hand, that it distinguishes those who live in cities or communities from people who live alone, and may therefore be inclined to be boorish. People who live together *have* to consider one another, or else they will forever be fighting.

There are lots of ways of showing politeness—in your looks, your gestures, your voice, but especially in your speech. "Hello" and "good-bye," "thank you" and "you're welcome" (or "don't mention it"), "please" and "excuse me" are among the most common of our polite expressions. They appear, in one form or another, in all civilized languages, and when you go to another country they are among the first things you learn.

"Hello" is a good old Anglo-Saxon term. It was originally "Hale be thou!"—a sort of blessing invoked upon the other person. People all over the world liked it so much that several languages besides English use it as a telephone greeting, French, German and Russian among them. But

Russian also has a telephone response that means "I'm listening!"—while Spanish says "What is it?"—and Italian says "Ready!" Practically all languages inquire after your health by some such expression as "How goes it?" or "How are you?"

"Good-bye" was at first "God be with you!"—again a sort of blessing. "Farewell" is not much heard these days, but it used to be common in the Middle Ages, often in the form "Fare you well!" It is still used in some Scandinavian tongues. "Adieu" is a word brought in by the Normans, and like the Spanish *adiós* of our Southwest, means "to God!" Several Slavic languages say "With God!"—while ancient Latin said "Be healthy!"—an expression that modern Russian uses for "hello." In French, German and Russian we find "Until we see each other again" (it's *au revoir* in French, *auf Wiedersehen* in German, *do svidanya* in Russian).

"Thank you" is connected with "think." The idea is that you are thinking with gratitude of the person who has done you a favor. German and Dutch, which are close to English, have the same expression, to which they often add "well." The German is *danke* or *danke schön*, while the Dutch is *dank U wel*. Latin used to say *gratias tibi ago* ("thanks to you I give"), and the *gratias* remains in Spanish *gracias* and Italian *grazie;* but French says *merci*, which is the same word as our "mercy," and Portuguese says *obrigado*, or "obliged." The most common Russian form is *spasibo*, which originally meant "may God save you!"

English is the only language that says "you're welcome" in reply to "thank you"; of course, English has other ways of saying it, like "don't mention it" or the "you bet!" that you often hear in the Midwest. German and Italian usually say "I beg" (with "you not to mention it" understood, but not said); French and Spanish say "there is nothing about which" (again "to speak" is understood); Russian says "not for that!" Here is the way these expressions look, but remember you'll have to get someone to pronounce them for you: German, *bitte* (or *bitte schön*); Italian, *prego*; French, *il n'y a pas de quoi;* Spanish, *no hay de que;* Russian, *nye za shto.*

"Please" started out as "if you please" or "if it please you," taken from the French *s'il vous plaît.* Spanish and Portuguese get around it by saying "do me the favor of" or "have the kindness to." German says "I beg," the same word it uses for "you're welcome." Italian has *per piacere* or *per favore.* Russian uses *pozhalsta,* with *zh* sounded like the *s* in *pleasure.*

For "excuse me" there is a variety of expressions, but there is also a trick for getting around it which works in most European countries; just say "pardon," which we, and everybody else, took from French.

Politeness involves the choice of certain terms and expressions in speaking to others. What may sound fairly polite in one language may not sound so at all in another. Our very common "give me" or "I want," when we go to a store, makes a bad impression in many countries, where it gives people the idea that you are ordering them about, or that "you want" regardless of how they feel about it. "I should like to have" or "would you please give me" works out much better, even at home. Some languages overdo "please," using it as a term of politeness even when they are not asking for anything in particular. Polish, for example, never says "sir," but "please, sir."

"Sir" reminds us that both we and others have worked out an entire series of what might be called handles to use in speaking to or about people in a polite way: "Sir,"

"Madam," "Mr.," "Mrs.," "Miss," and so forth, along with "Doctor," "Professor," "Colonel" and like terms that describe a person's calling and at the same time imply respect.

Here, by the way, is where we begin to notice differences in our own language. We would address a letter to "Mr. So-and-So," but the British would prefer "So-and-So, Esq.,"—the Esq., standing for Esquire, a term that you seldom hear in speech, but are forever running across in writing. It is the same word as Squire, and comes from a French word meaning "shield-bearer." It goes, of course, back to the days when knights had shield-bearers who were really apprentice knights, but had not yet gained their spurs or a title.

"Sir," on the other hand, was applied to the full-fledged knights, and in Britain is still used that way. But it has a strange story. It goes back to a Latin word *senior*, which meant "elder" (we still use the Latin word in that sense). "Elder" was not merely a distinction of age, but also a title of respect. An elder person is supposed to have gained wisdom from experience, and is at least entitled to be listened to; also, in medieval times, the elder brother inherited all of the family title and castle, while the younger brothers, called "cadets," often took up the army as a life career. So there was enough to make *senior*, or its descendant "sir," a title of respect. In Britain, they use it before a first name as an indication of the knight's rank (Sir Winston, or Sir Winston Churchill); otherwise, they use it exactly as we do, in addressing any man to whom they want to sound respectful without mentioning his name.

But *senior* had other curious developments. In a longer form, it also became *sire*, a title applied to kings. In French, it got attached to *mon*, meaning "my," and the two words together became *Monsieur*, the regular French word for either "sir" or "Mr." In Spanish it turned into *señor*, and in Italian into *signor*. Then the Spaniards and Italians thought of applying it also to women, and they got *señora* and *signora*, which mean "Madam," "Mrs." or "lady." This is a doubtful compliment, because ladies, when they reach a certain age, do not like to be reminded that they are "elders." But the funniest twist came when the Spaniards and Italians went on to apply it to young unmarried women by adding to *señor* and *signor* the endings *-ita* and *-ina*, which usually mean "small," and got *señorita* and *signorina*, which mean literally "little old woman." Fortunately, Spanish and Italian misses have forgotten all about the history of the word.

"Mister," "Mrs.," "Miss," "master" belong to another big family that starts out with Latin *magister*, "chief," "headman," a word applied, among other things, to the helmsman of a galley, or the man who beat time for the galley rowers. From this, he became on the one hand the "master" or "schoolmaster" (ancient schoolmasters often beat time as their pupils recited pieces from memory); this usage gives the Romance languages their word for "teacher," which is *maestro* in Spanish and Italian, *maître* in French; it even gives the German *Meister*. On the other hand, the *magister* was also the boss, or foreman, or master of the galley-slaves, so we get the other meaning of "master" as opposed to "servant" or "slave." Lastly, "master" was used as a title of respect to a superior, right before his name, and this, quickly pronounced, became "Mister." In the case of women, they added an ending *-ess*, which originally came from Greek, and this gives us "mistress" and "Mrs." "Mistress" was cut down to "Miss" for a young unmarried woman, but this happened not too long ago. In the days of Shakespeare people used "Mistress" for both married and unmarried women, and there are some today who claim it is unfair to give women away as being married or unmarried when we don't do the same thing for men, and urge that we go back to the universal "Mistress" of Shakespeare's time for all women.

In America, there is a good deal of use of "Mr.," "Mrs." and "Miss" without the person's name, as in "Mister, how far is it from here to city hall?"—or "How's the Mrs.?" This is not the best way in the world to use these words; it is better to say "Sir" than "Mister" if you don't know the man's name, and to inquire after the health of "your wife" or "Mrs. So-and-So."

Another big family of polite words comes from Latin *dominus*, "lord" or "master," and *domina*, "lady" or "mistress." French cut down *domina* to *dame*, a word that was passed on to us, and which the British use as the feminine of "sir" used as a knight's title. The French also put *ma*, "my" in front of *dame*, and got *madame*, the regular French word for both "lady" and "Mrs.," which came on to us in the form of "madam" or "ma'am." Lastly, the French gave *madame* an ending meaning "small" or "young," and turned it into *mademoiselle*, the regular French word for "Miss." The Spaniards and Italians took the masculine *dominus* and cut it down to *don*, which they use today before a man's first name as a title of address which is halfway between familiar and respectful. The Italians also took the feminine *domina* and turned it into *donna*, which is the regular Italian word for "woman," but may also be used as a title of respect, like "lady." Spanish *doña* is similarly used. You may notice that the original Latin *dominus* is connected with our own "dominate," which means "to lord it over."

The German form which corresponds to our "Mr." is

Herr, with *Frau* for "Mrs.," "lady," and *Fräulein* for "Miss." If you want to say "Sir" or "Madam" you say *mein Herr, meine Frau*, which works out just like the French *monsieur, madame*.

The Russians have words for "sir" and "madam," but at the present time they prefer to use other words which mean "citizen," "citizeness," and especially one word that means "comrade," *tovarishch;* strangely, this word comes from Turkish, and its earlier meaning is "apprentice."

There are few languages of civilized nations that don't use some sort of handle or other when their speakers want to address someone politely. Japanese has a word *san*, which is placed after the name and means indifferently "Mr.," "Mrs." or "Miss," so that Suzuki San may be Mr., Mrs., or Miss Suzuki.

"Lord" and "lady" are among the few titles or words of address that come down to us straight from Anglo-Saxon and were not brought in from Latin or French. But at first they had meanings you would hardly guess from the way they are used today. "Lord" was "loaf-warden," the man who stood guard over the loaf and handed out slices of bread to the family and retainers, and "lady" was "loaf-maid," the one who kneaded and baked the bread her husband distributed.

There is another matter connected with politeness which does not concern English so much as it does other languages. In English today we address just about everybody as "you." Also, we use "you" whether we are speaking to one person or to more than one, though some people occasionally say "you-all," or even "youse," if they are talking to several people at once. But we don't have to go very far back to discover that at one time "you" was used only for more than one person, along with "ye," and that in addressing a single person the customary forms were "thou" and "thee," which are still used in a good many sections of Britain and occasionally by the Quakers in America. How did "you" come to replace "thou" in talking to a single person? You give more importance to that one person if you imply that he represents others besides himself. So this shift from "thou" to "you" was really due to an effort to be polite.

Today, we still use a few additional polite forms, as when we say "Your Honor" to a judge, or "Your Excellency" to an ambassador, or when one Senator addresses another as "the gentleman from Virginia" instead of simply saying "Senator Byrd." In all these cases, there is also a shift from "are" to "is," "have" to "has," "see" to "sees" ("Your Honor is mistaken"; "Has Your Excellency seen this?"; "The gentleman from Virginia yields the floor?").

Most foreign languages indulge in the same antics, but to a far greater degree than we do. French, for instance, in speaking to one person, will use *tu*, "thou," if the person is a relative or a good friend, but *vous*, "you," if there is not too much familiarity. Spanish has *tú* for familiar address, but *Usted* for polite, and *Usted* comes from *Vuestra Merced*, which means "your grace," so if you are speaking politely in Spanish you are forever saying "Your Grace is" instead of "you are." Italian says "thou art" in familiar conversation, but either "you are" or "she is" in the polite. German has "they are" as a polite form of address for one person. And so it goes on and on, making you long for the good old days of Latin or Anglo-Saxon, when you said "thou art" to any single person, and "ye are" to any group, without having to worry about whether you were being polite or not.

In a few languages this business of politeness is carried over from "you" into "I." Instead of saying "I am," they will use something like "your servant is." English, by the way, is the only language that spells "I" with a capital, while many languages use a capital for the word they use as a polite "you." This looks as though the English speaker had too big a sense of his own importance; actually, the capital we use for "I" is just a flourish that the scribes in the Middle Ages used when the letter *I* stood alone.

The use of polite words and forms of address does not really add anything to your meaning, which gets across whether you are polite or not. It does, though, serve to show that you are considerate of the person you are talking to, and that you want him to know you are thinking about him and not just of yourself.

This does not prevent funny situations from arising. Not only foreigners who come to Italy, but the Italians themselves often get all tangled up in their three different ways of addressing one person. Spaniards, who use "thou" or "Your Grace" to one person, generally prefer "Your Graces" when speaking to more than one, even on familiar terms. It is amusing to hear a Spanish mother speaking to her children in this fashion: "Your Graces have been naughty today, and so Your Graces will go to bed without their suppers."

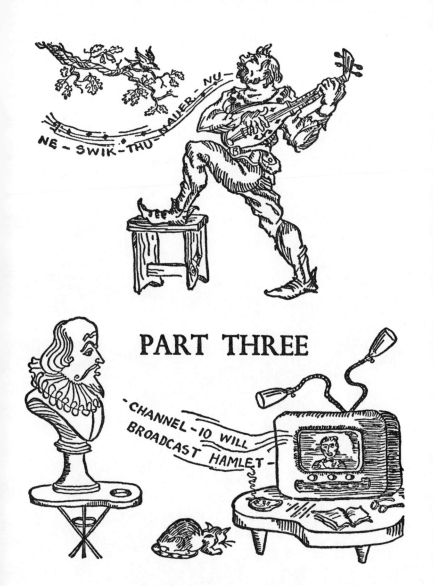

PART THREE

OUR LANGUAGE

1 *How English Grew*

THE ENGLISH LANGUAGE WAS ONCE THE tongue of the Angles, Saxons and Jutes who came to England across the North Sea in the fifth century A.D. Before that time, Britain had been inhabited by people who spoke a Celtic tongue, very close to present-day Welsh. The Celtic Britons, however, had been conquered by the Romans in the first century A.D., and we have every reason to believe that a great many of them spoke Latin as well as Celtic when the Anglo-Saxons arrived.

The Britons and the Anglo-Saxons did not mix very well, and neither did their languages. Anglo-Saxon on British soil therefore remained pretty much what it had been when its speakers still lived on the continent of Europe—a Germanic tongue, closely linked to what was later to become German, and even more closely related to the ancestor of present-day Dutch.

But changes were occurring all the time. For one thing, the Anglo-Saxons, while they were still on the continent of Europe, had come in contact with other Germanic tribes that had been in touch with the Romans, and from them they had acquired words like "street" and "cheese," which is how the Anglo-Saxons pronounced Latin *strata* and *caseus*. For another, the Anglo-Saxons, who had been pagans when they landed in England, were converted to Christianity. The language of the Christian Church in the western part of Europe was Latin, and this meant that additional words from that language began to filter into the speech of the Anglo-Saxons, words like "plant," "pear," "sack," coming from Latin *planta, pira, saccus*. The Latin of the western Church had been previously penetrated by many Greek words, because Greek was the original language of the New Testament. So many Greek words which had passed into Latin later passed on into Anglo-Saxon. Among these were "angel," which in Greek had the form *angelos* and the meaning of "messenger," and which in Latin had become *angelus*; "bishop," which comes from Greek *episcopos*, "overseer" (the bishop is the overseer of his diocese or flock); even "church" itself, which is Greek *kyriakon*, "belonging to the Lord" (the people of Scotland, who keep the old pronunciation, still say "kirk").

But besides Latin and Greek, there was another tongue that made deep inroads into the speech of the Anglo-Saxons. The Danes, whose homeland was further north than the places along the European North Sea coast where the Anglo-Saxons had come from, were great rovers and fighters. Along with their kinsmen the Norwegians and the Swedes, they formed the Scandinavian branch of the Germanic-speaking peoples—very closely related among themselves, a little more distantly to the speakers of Anglo-Saxon, German and Dutch, and much more distantly connected with the speakers of Latin, Greek and Celtic.

These Danish seafarers, or Vikings, began to make raids and settlements on the northeastern coast of England. At first the Anglo-Saxons tried to drive them back, then they decided that they might as well accept them and merge with them. The language of the Danes and that of the Anglo-Saxons were not too dissimilar, but there were some pretty important differences. These were simply merged, and the language of the Anglo-Saxons became richer thereby. It is surprising what common, everyday words in modern English are not Anglo-Saxon, but Danish. When you say "They are ill" you are using pure Danish. When you say "Take the knife and cut the steak," the only Anglo-Saxon words you are using are "the" and "and"; the rest is Danish.

For a century or two, Angles, Saxons, Jutes and Danes lived side by side, merging into an English nation that was ruled over by such men as King Alfred, a Saxon, and King Canute (it really should be spelled Cnut), a Dane. Then trouble came to England, but it was trouble that in the long run proves that "all's well that ends well."

Other Scandinavians, or Norsemen, similar to the Danes, had invaded France just as the Danes had invaded England. They had finally gotten settled in the northwestern corner of France, a region called Normandy, or land of the Northmen, after them. During the century or more that followed their settlement on French soil, they dropped their Scandinavian language and adopted French, along with French manners and customs. One Scandinavian trait they did not drop, and that was the desire to conquer and rule. About the middle of the eleventh century, their leader, William, decided that he needed broader lands to rule over, and he began to cast covetous eyes upon the large and prosperous Kingdom of England. The Anglo-Saxons and Danes, by this time, had fastened upon "English" and "England" as suitable names for themselves and their country. In 1066, Duke William of Normandy crossed the Straits of Dover and landed at Hastings with a large army, made up not only of his own Normans, but of adventurers from every part of western Europe. The Saxon king, Harold, met him in battle. The fight was long and furious, for the English were hardy and desperate in defense of their own homes. The Normans, however, had superior strategy and made better use of their forces, particularly their archers, whose arrows played havoc in the Saxon ranks. Finally, King Harold himself fell mortally wounded, with an arrow in his eye. This was the signal for the Saxon rout and the Norman victory. William and his Normans had made themselves masters of England.

It was not so easy for the English-speaking Saxons and the French-speaking Normans to merge, as the Anglo-Saxons and Danes had merged previously. For about two centuries, the English population and the Norman overlords considered themselves separate, and each spoke his own language. Finally, the weight of numbers told. The Norman nobility gave way and adopted the English of the bulk of the population, and from about 1400 on, there was but one England, one English people, and one English language.

But we should not think that the triumph of English over French was a one-way affair. At the same time that the Norman conquerors adopted English, they put into it a tremendous number of their own French words. There is one word that you use at every turn, "very." "Very" is French, and in the form used by the Normans it was *verai*. Modern French still uses the word, in the form *vrai*, but in modern French it means "true." You can see the connection: "I am truly sorry," "I am very sorry." You might ask at this point: "What was the word the Anglo-Saxons used for 'very'?" It's a word that you still use, but in a different meaning, "sore." If you read older works of literature, you will come across such expressions as "I am sore vexed," "I am sore wroth." That is probably the way we should be using it today if the Norman Conquest had not taken place.

Or take the word "pay." This is the French *payer*, brought in by the Normans. French, by the way, had taken it from Latin *pacare*, "to appease," "to pacify," the idea being that the best way to appease somebody, or keep him at peace, is to "pay" him off. Here again, what did the Saxons use before the coming of the Normans? Again, it's a word you use all the time, but in a different sense, "tell." Have you ever noticed that in a bank you have a paying teller and a receiving teller? Does the teller tell anything, in the modern sense? No, he counts money and pays it. He gets his name from the old Anglo-Saxon use of "tell." If you need further proof, consider that "tell" belongs to the same family of words as "toll." You know what a toll-bridge is: one where you pay to get across.

By the fourteenth century, English as we know it today was fully formed. Its first great writer was Chaucer, the author of *Canterbury Tales*. When you try to read Chaucer you encounter some difficulty, but by and large you can understand him, and you recognize his language as your own. If you take writers before Chaucer, you will have to study their language, almost as you would have to study a foreign language—say German or Dutch. What is it, then, that gives Chaucer's English its modern flavor? It's just what you would expect: the mixture of the Normans' French with the old language of the Anglo-Saxons and Danes. Once this mixture takes place, the language becomes pretty much as we know it.

Of course, it still sounds very ancient, and even funny in spots. There is an old song about the coming of summer and the singing of the cuckoo that goes back to the days of Chaucer; it starts: "Sumer is icumen in," which you can figure out, and ends: "Ne swik thu nauer nu," which you can't (it means: "Be thou not silent now").

For about two centuries after Chaucer, the language just grew and grew. It added many new words, because with the invention of printing people began to be able to read and write in greater numbers than before, when all writing had to be done by hand, and books became more numerous. One result was that people became curious about the old languages of western civilization, Latin and Greek. As they studied them, they picked out words they fancied, gave them an English twist, and stuck them into their own writings. So we get, in addition to the Latin and Greek words adopted back in the days of King Alfred, and those brought in with the French of William the Conqueror, a large and growing number of words simply picked out of the Latin and Greek dictionaries and appropriated for English use. Consider, for instance, "bishop" and "episcopal." The first, as we saw, was the Greek word for "overseer," carried from Greek into Latin, then into Anglo-Saxon; but "episcopal" is a word that comes into the language later, in pretty much the Greek-Latin form. "Priest" was at one time the Greek *presbyter*, "elder," adopted by Latin; then, as Latin words were adopted by Anglo-Saxon, *presbyter* became *preost* and English, as time went on, made it "priest"; but in the later centuries between Chaucer and Shakespeare, they came across *presbyter* in the Greek and Latin dictionaries, adopted it all over again, and made it into "Presbyterian." Latin had a word *fragilis*, meaning "easy to break"; in French, *fragilis* turned into *frêle*, and English took it from French as "frail"; but later, seeing *fragilis* in the dictionaries, the writers decided they wanted it, and adopted it as "fragile."

These Greek and Latin words, brought in since the days of Chaucer, supply us with the more learned, literary and scientific part of our vocabulary. They are usually longer than either the native Anglo-Saxon-Danish words or the French words of the Normans, and they are usually quite close in appearance to the Latin and Greek originals. This process of appropriating Latin and Greek words and using them for modern purposes goes on at a fast pace even to-day. Take words like "atom" or "anti-biotic." They are formed out of straight Greek. "Atom" is *a*, meaning "not," plus *tomos*, meaning "cut": "what you can't cut," what is indivisible; it happens to be a misnomer, for modern science has found a way to break up the atom. "Anti-biotic" is *anti*, "against," plus *bios*, "life," "what is against, or kills off, all germ life." There is really no limit or end to the number of words that can be put together on the basis of Latin and Greek roots, and this means that our vocabulary, although shaped around a hard Germanic core, gets more Greek and Latin all the time.

In the sixteenth century the greatest poet of the English language, Shakespeare, composed his many plays and works, and a very short time later the King James version of the Bible saw the light. The language of Shakespeare and the Bible, while it sounds a little ancient in spots, is thoroughly understandable to the reader of today. In fact, many present-day writers try to model their writings on the works of Shakespeare and the language of the King James Bible.

The early seventeenth century saw the English language transplanted to American shores. English was in those days a comparatively small language, with about five million speakers, fewer than those of French, German, Spanish or Italian. What gave it the impulse to become a great and widespread language was its going out to other continents, particularly America and Australia. Today, of the 250 or more million speakers of English, only 55 million or so live in the British Isles, while the United States claims three times that number.

Another effect of the movement of English speakers to

other shores was that the language, which until the beginning of the seventeenth century had grown up only in England, now began to grow up in different places and, naturally enough, in different directions. The Englishmen who went off to America or Australia found themselves in a different environment, with different objects and actions to name. These objects and actions had already been named by the people who had lived in America and Australia before them. What was more natural than for the displaced Englishmen to take these strange new words into their own language, just as the objects came into their experience? And it was just as natural for them to pass on both objects and names for them to their kinsmen back at home. So the English language began to be enriched with the words of the American Indians and the Australian natives—"squaw," "tomahawk," "wigwam" on the one hand, "boomerang," "kangaroo," "billabong" on the other.

Then the American and Australian settlers began to coin words on their own, and pass them on to their British cousins, in return for the new words that the British went on coining and passing out to the colonies. As the colonies, particularly the American ones, which became an independent nation, grew in size, population and importance, the language exchange across the oceans became greater and greater. Today, it is likely that more new words and expressions are contributed to the common language by the Americans than by the British and their Dominions. This is quite natural, because we now have nearly twice as many speakers of English as they.

In the nineteenth and twentieth centuries especially, English has been growing by leaps and bounds. It has grown in territorial extent, with new and undeveloped lands like our own former Wild West and the Australian bush becoming settled with English speakers. It has grown in population, with the number of speakers doubling since 1900. It has grown in power and influence, with many people of other lands and languages learning to speak English for purposes of trade, travel and culture. It has grown in richness of vocabulary and expressiveness, with thousands upon thousands of new words being added to the language's treasure house by the discoveries of science and the inventiveness of the speakers.

Today, as we write, English is a leader among the world's languages. It is officially spoken in lands covering one-fifth of the earth's surface, by populations numbering roughly one-tenth of the total population of the globe. It is widely distributed, and serves at the same time the purposes of commerce, science, culture and general communication. It has far outstripped its earlier rivals, French, Spanish, Italian, German; and even though new rivals, such as Russian, Chinese and Hindustani have appeared, they are still in no position to challenge the supremacy of English.

We must, however, remember that languages, like human beings, are not eternal. They not only are born and grow and develop. They also wither and sicken and die. The Roman living in the days of the Emperor Augustus would probably have laughed at the notion that his Latin tongue would one day become a language not popularly spoken throughout the known world. A similar fate could overtake English. In fact, it probably will. This will not be in itself a calamity, since languages have a way of leaving their own heirs and replacements behind them, just as Latin left its children, the Romance languages.

On the other hand, the decay and disappearance of the English language is a process that we, its speakers, ought not to try to hasten. We should rather wish our language which is now in the full glory of its prime, to live on to a ripe, fruitful old age.

Is there anything we can do about this? Yes, a good deal. There is such a thing as preserving the language, keeping it from abuse and mistreatment, handling it as a dear and treasured friend rather than as something to be kicked around.

This we shall see later. But first, let us look at this language of ours as it exists today, in the many shapes that it takes on in the various parts of the world where it is spoken.

2 *The Geography of English*

GEOGRAPHICALLY SPEAKING, OUR ENGLISH tongue extends all over the globe. It is to be found in each of the five continents and in that vast island world that stretches across the broad Pacific. On it the sun never sets.

But it would be strange indeed if such a far-flung language were to be spoken everywhere without differences and variations. Actually, there are as many local varieties of English as there are localities where English is spoken. The language of New York may be close to, but it is not quite the same as the language of Philadelphia, a city that you can reach from New York in a little over an hour. The New Yorker will tell you that a certain place is three blocks away, the Philadelphian that it is three squares away. The New Yorker will tell you to stay on the sidewalk, the Philadelphian will ask you to stay on the pavement. If you are hungry, the New Yorker may offer you a hero sandwich, the Philadelphian a hoagy.

If you are a careful observer, you will notice that each city has its little individual ways of expressing certain things. Then, in addition to word-differences, you may also notice some sound-differences. If you live in the East, you know that you pronounce "Mary," "marry" and "merry" differently. Now get someone who comes from the Midwest (say Omaha or Indianapolis), and ask him to pronounce those three words. You will be surprised to hear him sounding all three of them exactly alike. Or you may be accustomed to pronounce "greasy" as though there were a *z* in the word instead of an *s*, and it will surprise you to notice that someone from another locality pronounces it *greassy*. You may hear *boid* instead of "bird" in some people's pronunciation. All these are local, geographical differences.

In addition to an almost infinite number of local differences, there are three major areas of difference in speech in the United States. One area takes in New England, New Jersey, Delaware, Maryland, and the eastern parts of New York and Pennsylvania. Another takes in the southern states from Virginia to Florida and from the Atlantic coast to Texas. The third takes in the rest of the country, from the Alleghanies to the Pacific, and from the Canadian border to the Ohio River and on beyond the Mississippi. These three big varieties of American speech are called Eastern, Southern, and General American or Midwestern. One easy way of telling a Midwestern speaker is by the way he sounds his final *r*'s in words like "father." The East and South say *fathuh;* the West says *fatherrr*. The South distinguishes itself from the North and West by sounding words like "egg" and "leg" as though they were spelled *aig* and *laig;* Southern speakers are also apt to say "you-all" when speaking to more than one person.

All these differences and many, many more besides make for variety in our American speech, and variety is the spice of life. But it must be remembered that these differences in our American speech are few and unimportant when we compare them with similar differences in other lands, like Italy or China, where people speaking two different dialects don't understand each other at all. At least we all manage to understand one another.

Also, in American speech there is no superiority of one

THE ENGLISH LANGUAGE AROUND THE WORLD

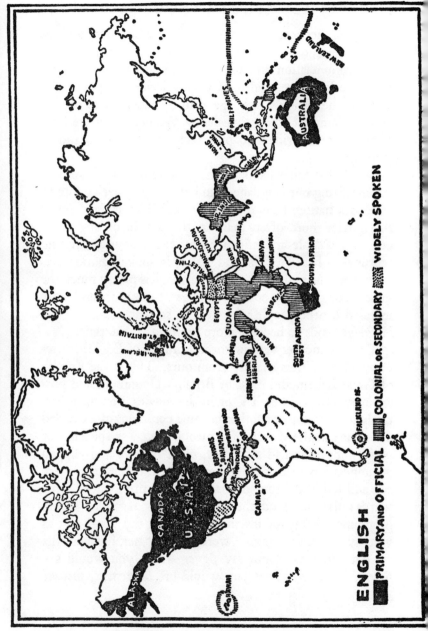

ENGLISH

PRIMARY AND OFFICIAL   COLONIAL or SECONDARY   WIDELY SPOKEN

variety or accent over another. The Midwesterner, the Southerner and the New Englander are each entitled to his own pronunciation and use of words. In some countries there are language academies which decide what local variety of the nation's language shall be accepted as official, and condemn all others as dialects. We believe in the freedom of the individual to pick and use his own brand of language.

But on the other hand, we have more unofficial ways of standardizing our language than have most other countries. We, as a nation, have more radio and TV sets and go to the movies more often than do the people of any other country. People are influenced by the pronunciation and words they hear on radio and TV or in spoken motion pictures, and our radio-TV-movie language is pretty much the same throughout the country, and gets to be more and more imitated by the people who hear it, so that our American language tends to become more uniform all the time.

There is another very important branch of English, however, which differs sharply from ours. This is the English of Great Britain and most of Britain's Dominions and possessions. On radio or TV or in the movies, you have certainly at one time or another become conscious of a decided difference in the speech of someone who was speaking or performing. He had a sharper, more incisive and clipped pronunciation than most of our American speakers, more rise and fall in the tone of his voice. He pronounced some words differently from the way an American speaker would pronounce them; for instance, he would say "pot" not as you say it, but as though it were spelled *pawt*, but with the *aw* cut short; he might say *figger* where you would say *figure*, *leftenant* where you would use *lieutenant*, *shedule* where you would say *schedule*. Or he would stress "laboratory" on the *bor* instead of on the *lab*, or use unfamiliar expressions like "wage packet," "underground," "joint," which you somehow figured meant "pay envelope," "subway," "roast." And he would use such exclamations as "Wizard!" or "Smashing!" Yes, he was a Britisher, speaking the best European variety of English, the "King's English" of Britain and her Empire. In books written by Britons and printed in Britain, you may have come across unfamiliar spellings like "kerb," "tyre," "jewellery," "programme," "defence," "labour," for what to you are "curb," "tire," "jewelry," "program," "defense," "labor." These different spellings of words that they pronounce pretty much as we do are also part of the King's English.

Here again, there is no superiority of one version of English over the other. The British can certainly justify their speech on the ground that their country had it first, and that they live on its home soil. We can justify ours on the ground that we have the absolute majority of all English speakers, and that in many ways our speech comes closer to the English of Queen Elizabeth the First and Shakespeare than does the modern King's English, which in some respects has changed while ours has stayed more as it was when the first English settlers came to America.

In spite of all the differences, there is no real contradiction or lack of understanding between British and American English. They are merely two branches of the same tongue, differing from each other only a little more, if at all, than two different varieties of American English or two different varieties of British English. Because on British soil, although the country is much smaller than ours, the difference in dialects is far more marked than it is with us. While the King's English is standard in Britain, there are many local varieties. There is, for example, the Cockney dialect, spoken by the lower classes in the city of London, which is at least as far removed from the cultured King's English of the British Broadcasting Corporation as the lower-class speech of Brooklyn or the Bronx is from the good American of our own radio announcers. There are dialects in Yorkshire, Devonshire, the English Midlands, the south of England, that differ from one another more than our Southern, Eastern and General American. There is a Scottish ʼway of speaking English which you will find in the poems of Bobbie Burns, and an Irish variety of English that you can often hear on the lips of New York policemen and bus drivers. There is a super-refined Oxford accent which produces as artificial an effect, in its own way, as does the pronunciation of some of our own stage stars.

Then we have the languages of the British Dominions. Canada is geographically closer to the United States than it is to Britain, and the result is that the English of Canada sounds far more like an American than like a British dialect (in fact, Englishmen are forever accusing Canadians of speaking with an American accent). Yet once in a while a Britishism creeps into the tongue of Canada. During the war, for instance, draft authorities of Canada and the U. S. fixed on a unique way of telling whether a man was a Canadian or an American. They would ask him to recite the alphabet. When he came to the last letter, if he was an American he would say "zee"; but if he was a Canadian, he would pronounce it "zed," English fashion.

Australia and New Zealand were settled mainly by lower-class Englishmen from the south of England, with the result that their speech comes close to the London Cockney (*lidy* for "lady," for instance). But in addition, the Australians and New Zealanders, being active, energetic people, like the Americans, have been busy creating a language of their own, built in part on words borrowed from the Australian natives and the New Zealand Maori, in part on their own imagination and experiences. New Zealand, for example, uses *kiwi* for "doughboy" and *kapai!* for "Atta boy!"—both borrowed from the Polynesian language of the Maori; it also says *up stick* for "to move house." Australians use *cooee*, a word taken from the natives, as a long-distance "yoohoo," while they speak of "blackfellow's gift" in the sense of our "Indian giver"; they use "to shout" in the meaning of "to treat," and they "bot some oscar from a cobber" where we would "borrow some money from a pal." Hard work goes by the slang name of *graft* or *yakka* in both countries, which also "chew the rag" in the sense of "brooding over something" and say "cow" for "no good."

In South Africa, the English settlers found a white population that had already settled before them. These were the Boers, who had come from Holland and spoke Dutch. In the course of time, however, their Dutch had changed to the point where it could be described as a new language, to which they gave the name of Afrikaans. The English of South Africa is interlarded with words and terms borrowed from Afrikaans on the one hand, from the native Negro languages, like Zulu, on the other. Here are a couple of picturesque terms from South African English: "We shall trek over the veld at schimmel day" ("We shall start journeying over the plain at dawn"); "Shall we sit on the stoop long?" ("Shall we sit on the stoop for a while?")

The British in India, while they continued to speak the 's English, gave it numerous words and terms borrowed from the native languages (Hindustani, Bengali, Tamil, etc.). This led to an Anglo-Indian, or Hobson-Jobson, samples of which are "to dumb-cow" for "to brow-beat" and "bahadur" for "stuffed shirt." Some of the Anglo-Indian words got into regular English; among them are "bungalow," "mango," "curry" and "tiffin."

Last of all, there is a variety, or rather a series of varieties, of English to which one sometimes wonders whether the name of English should be applied at all. As the British traders scoured the seas, they came across numerous populations with which they had no common language. This state of affairs seems to have first come up with the Chinese in ports like Hong Kong and Shanghai. Driven by the urge to do business, the traders began to use with the Chinese a compromise language, in which English and Chinese were mingled, with English contributing most of the words and Chinese contributing the order of words and the language imagery. This made-to-order language was called "Business English," but the Chinese could not pronounce "business" and turned it into "pidgin." The habit of using Pidgin then spread from the China coasts to the islands of the southern Pacific, where new compromise languages were formed with the Melanesians of the Fiji and Solomons Islands, the blackfellows of Australia, the natives of New Guinea. Other Pidgin languages began to flourish along the West African coast. While the British were doing this, we were developing our own type of American Indian Pidgin, though we did not call it by that name, for communication with the Indians. Sentences like "Heap big chief go tepee, see squaw, papoose" would fit well into the Pidgin class. It may be added that not only English Pidgins were created by the traders, but also French, Spanish and Portuguese Pidgins—in fact as many Pidgins as there are European languages that have come in contact with native tongues of Asia, Africa, America or the islands.

Here are a few samples of English Pidgin varieties, all showing the same basic features—the use of English words along with native habits of thought and speech, and, occasionally, native words:

Chinese-English Pidgin—"cow-child" for "girl," "bull-child" for "boy," "have-got-wata-top-side" for "crazy."

Melanesian-English Pidgin—"man belong bullamacow" for "butcher"; "put clothes belong-a table" for "set the table"; "shoot 'im kaikai" for "serve the dinner."

West African-English Pidgin—"Who dat man?" for "Who goes there?"

No one knows exactly how many people speak varieties of Pidgin English, but the number has been estimated as high as thirty million.

We should not, of course, forget the many educated continental Europeans, Asiatics, Africans and Latin Americans who have learned English, either in the schools or as a result of travel and business, and handle it well, though usually with a foreign accent. For continental Europe alone, it is estimated that over five million people to whom English is not the mother-tongue speak it well. The government of India claims that at least twenty-five million of the country's native population speak English, and this, it says, places India as the third greatest English-speaking nation in the world, following immediately after the United States and Great Britain, and ahead of Canada, Australia, New Zealand or South Africa.

Population figures are forever shifting and changing, and figures for the speakers of languages with them. As we write, however, this seems to be the approximate score for English speakers throughout the world:

Continental United States (where practically everyone speaks English, although at least 20 million of our people were born abroad)	160,000,000
American possessions (Alaska, Hawaii, Puerto Rico, Virgin Islands, Canal Zone, etc.)	2,000,000
Great Britain, Northern Ireland, Eire (where most of the population speaks English), British possessions in Europe (Malta, Gibraltar)	55,000,000
Canada	15,000,000
British possessions in the Western Hemisphere (Bahamas, Bermuda, British Guiana, British Honduras, etc.)	1,000,000
British possessions in Asia (Cyprus, Malaya, Hong Kong, etc.)	1,000,000
Australia and New Zealand	10,000,000
British possessions in the Pacific	1,000,000
Union of South Africa and British possessions in Africa	5,000,000
Total	250,000,000

To this total of native speakers of English may be added at least 50 million cultured foreigners in Europe, Latin America, Asia (particularly India, Pakistan, Ceylon and Burma) and in Oceania (particularly the Philippines), plus perhaps another 30 million speakers of English Pidgins.

From these very rough, very approximate figures, several important facts stand out:

1. English is the mother-tongue of about 250 million people, or one out of every ten of the earth's inhabitants.

2. English is widely distributed all over the globe.

3. English has not only a native population, but also a very large and international foreign following, whose size

can only be guessed at, but which seemingly ranges between 50 and 100 million additional people, bringing the
total number of English speakers up to between 300 and
350 million, or one out of every seven or eight persons living in the world today.

The geography of English is one of the miracles of our
modern age. Here is a language which at the beginning of
the seventeenth century was current only in the British
Isles, and which has now expanded to the point where it
appears in almost every corner of the globe, and is spoken
by almost every color and race under the sun. It is indeed
a language to be proud of.

3 The Byways of English

DIALECTS ARE A MATTER OF GEOGRAPHY. Slang is nationwide. There are some who think that only poorer and less educated people use slang. This is not necessarily true. A little bit of slang, in fact, is used by practically everybody. Slang is a departure from standard, accepted language, but it may easily turn into standard language if it meets with enough favor. Or it may die out and leave little or no trace.

Take, for example, the current expression "scram." Thirty years ago it was unknown and unheard-of. What they had in its place in those days was something you have probably never heard: "Twenty-three-skiddoo." The origin of the "twenty-three" part is quite mysterious. In French, they had previously used "twenty-two" with about the same meaning. "Skiddoo" seems to have something to do with "skid," or an earlier slang "skedaddle," followed by an ending -*oo* that is probably of Australian native origin (as in "kangaroo"), and that we find applied today to new slang words, like "twisteroo." "Scram" could perhaps be a shortened form of "scramble." The point is that "skiddoo" has just about vanished from the scene, and "scram" may follow it into the junkheap in another twenty years or so, and be replaced by something entirely different. Or it may remain, and become part of the regular language. Today, we don't consider words like "fireworks" or "hubbub" as slang, but they were so considered once, until Shakespeare used them in his works and gave them full standing. Other words that were once slang are "clumsy" and "strenuous," and certainly no one objects to them today.

English is a language very rich in slang, but the mortality among slang words is very high. People who make up our dictionaries usually admit slang expressions on probation. They are either placed in a separate section of the dictionary, or marked "colloquial" or "vulgar" or "slang." If they survive a certain number of years, the label is removed, and they are admitted on a basis of equality with other words. If they disappear from use, they vanish also from the dictionaries.

Some of our slang originates here, some in Britain. Just as there is an interchange of regular words, so there is an interchange of slang between the two countries. "Corny," "whodunit," "jitterbug," "jalopy," "jerk" are American, but "fed up," "wind up," "swank" started in Britain.

"Ain't" is one of our oldest slang words. It started in Britain, and was given currency by King Charles II. But slang is far older than that, and quite international. In Latin, the word for "head" was *caput*, from which we get a large number of words, "cape," "capital," "capitol" and "captain" among them. But the Romans were not satisfied with their regular word for "head." They began to use in its place *testa*, which meant "jug." This slang use became so widespread that by the time Latin turned into French and Italian we find the descendants of *testa* used as frequently as those of *caput* with the meaning of "head." In Italian, both *testa* and *capo* are used today, but French prefers *tête*, while *caput*, which became *chief* in Old French, and then passed on to English (what is a chief, but a head-man?), later on developed into *chef* (the man who is at the "head" of an enterprise, particularly a kitchen). If we explore farther back, we find that ancient Sanskrit used a word that meant "pot" as a slang term for "head," which reminds you of our "crackpot." "To get someone's goat" may strike you as typical twentieth-century American slang; yet we find this very same expression, with the same meaning, in the writings of a great sixteenth-century French scholar.

Some words are plain slang. Others are halfway between slang and normal. Terms like "soap opera," "getaway," "comeback" are in this doubtful class. Some of our slang comes from foreign sources. Our use of "fresh" in the sense of "impudent" comes from German *frech*, while "kibitzer" comes from Yiddish. "Fake" and "faker" come from Arabic *faqīr*, which means "poor"; but in eastern countries a poor man or beggar is often also a holy man, who performs strange stunts, such as causing a rope to stand up in the air; some westerners choose to view these seeming miracles as plain parlor tricks, hence a *faqīr* becomes a "faker," and his stunt a "fake."

In a good many cases, slang words and uses can be traced to one individual. Dizzy Dean, of baseball fame, is responsible for "goodasterous" as the opposite of "disastrous," and "slud" as the past of "slide." Walter Winchell started the expression "making whoopee," and Shakespeare himself was the first to use, at least in writing, "beat it" and "not so hot." But far more often the creator of the slang expression is unknown.

One feature of slang is its creation of many words for the same thing. "Dollar," for instance, will appear as "buck," "simoleon," "iron man," "toadskin," "smacker" and a dozen other expressions. But the very fact that there are so many words contending for the same meaning weakens most of them, so that they fall by the wayside.

English slang is picturesque, and appeals to the imagination. The slang current in other languages works out the same way. French, for instance, has words that literally mean "camel" or "calf" to indicate that a person is stupid, and the bill that the waiter brings you at the end of your restaurant meal is known as "the sorrowful one." Spanish calls a pest a "calamity," and uses "to scalp" or "to take the hair off somebody" in the sense of "to kid someone along." "Chicken" in Spanish is slangily used for a handsome, dashing young man.

Slang, as we said before, is nationwide. The expressions we have been using would be understood pretty much anywhere in America. Dialect is local, as where sections of the Midwest use "mango" in the sense of "green pepper." Two other items that call for discussion are cant and jargon. Jargon is a form of speech current in a given class or profession and hardly understood on the outside. Cant, the language of the underworld, is a variety of jargon. A French poet of the fifteenth century, François Villon, used in many of his poems a type of Paris underworld cant that cannot be understood today. American and British cant has been mysterious in the past, but today large segments of it are known, having been spread by detective stories, and many of its expressions have become general slang and even regular language. "Sawbuck" for "$10" and "grand" for "$1,000" are generally understood and even used, though they are not the best language in the world. Other cant expressions that have acquired a measure of respectability are "take the rap," "take for a ride," "throw the book at," "blow one's top," "frisk," "gat." But there are many others not so well known, like "quizmaster" for "District Attorney."

There are jargons of the various professions and trades, even jargons of the sexes and age-levels. Bankers, lawyers, doctors will talk among themselves in specialized languages which people on the outside have difficulty following. So do scientists, technicians, teachers, scholars in every field. But it is not only the intellectual professions that have jargons, it is also the manual trades and occupations. From them, too, many words have come into the general language. Shipboard terminology is very extensive and complicated, as you know if you have read stories about ships, particularly the old sailing vessels. When you speak of "knowing the ropes," "keeping on an even keel," "keeping a weather eye open," "giving plenty of leeway," you are using sailors' expressions that have become general. But there are many more such expressions that have not entered the general language, and that you have to look up in the dictionary if you want to understand all the details of a sea story.

There is a military jargon, with separate branches for each of the services. There is a railroad men's jargon, with terms like "reefer," "doghouse," "brain cage," "monkey wagon." Rodeo people have introduced to the language terms like "jughead" (originally a stubborn horse) and "grab the apple" (hold on to the saddle horn). Truck drivers speak of "pinning her ears back" for gliding to a slow stop, "eating gravel" for having to make a detour, "tap dancer" for a retail delivery wagon. Soda fountain attendants have been known to coin terms like "stretch one and paint it red" for a large Coke with a cherry. There is no occupation that doesn't have its own special terminology, which baffles outsiders.

The sexes and age-levels have their own jargons, too. Girls and women will use terms like "hankie" and "yummy," which boys and men will avoid; also, they will have an entire range of colors, like "beige," "ecru," "taupe," "mauve," which mean little or nothing to the masculine gender. Boys in return have a sporting terminology which stumps the girls, at least once in a while.

Young people often devise a language of their own which the older generation has difficulty in understanding. But the teen-age language changes and shifts with such startling rapidity that it is almost hopeless to try to keep abreast of it. "Bratting" for baby-sitting, "his garden is green" for "he has money," "bubble" for one who is too conceited, "cooking with gas" for "getting along well," may or may not be in style by the time this book appears.

Coming back to general usage, there is a form of slang (at least it was slang in the beginning) which consists of cutting down and abbreviating long words, or using their initials, as when one says "math" for "mathematics," "eke" for "economics," or "G. S." for "general science." These forms are still somewhat frowned upon, but many similar ones are fully accepted; in fact, in a great many cases the original longer form is all but forgotten. "Cab," for instance, comes from "cabriolet," an originally French word meaning "little goat" and applied to a conveyance that leaped and bounded over the cobblestones; "mob" is an abbreviation of *mobile vulgus*, Latin for "fickle crowd." In both these words, it is the initial part that was selected; but in "van" from "caravan" and "wig" from "periwig" it is the ending; while in "flu" from "influenza" and "skeet" from "mosquito" it's the middle part. "Bus" comes from "omnibus," a Latin word that means "for everybody." Once in a while, abbreviations lead to confusion. When you say "gas," do you mean the gas from your kitchen range, or are you abbreviating the "gasoline" you use in your car tank?

The language of initials may likewise be confusing.

"G.I." in the army is a soldier, but in medicine it stands for "gastro-intestinal," the sort of X-ray examination that covers your digestive tract. To us, "U.S.A." means "United States of America," but to the South African it stands for "Union of South Africa." "B.C." stands for "before Christ"; you would expect "A.C.," "after Christ," to be its opposite; instead, you get "A.D.," which stands for *Annus Domini*, Latin for "Year of the Lord." "R.S.V.P.," which you find on many invitation cards, stands for French *répondez s'il vous plaît*, "answer, please," and means that your hostess wants to know from you whether or not you will attend the party.

Many of our abbreviated forms appear only in writing. You write "lbs." and pronounce "pounds." Just what does the "lbs." stand for? The Latin for "pound" is *libra*, and "lb." is its abbreviation; to it, an English -*s* is added to make it plural. This is not very rational, nor is the abbreviation "cwt." for "hundredweight," where the *c.* abbreviates Latin *centum*, "hundred," and the *wt.* abbreviates English "weight." But language goes by custom rather than by reason. Why "Xmas" for "Christmas"? The X is not an X at all, but the first Greek letter (which in our alphabet would have to appear as two letters, *CH*) of Greek *Christos*, "Christ."

Here are a few very twentieth-century abbreviations which will test your knowledge of international affairs: UN, UNESCO, USSR, POW. An older one, which you will see on the caps of British sailors, is HMS. If you can give the correct reading for all of them, you deserve a prize.

Usually words lead to abbreviations. It is rare for the opposite to take place, and for an abbreviation to lead to a word. The one case we can think of is the theatrical "cue." It stands for the letter Q, which in turn is the abbreviation of Latin *quando*, "when," used in old scripts to indicate that the actor was to begin his lines (a little bit like our "say when").

Abbreviations are largely, but not entirely, international. If you find yourself in a French, Spanish or Italian-speaking country, and you want cold water, don't turn on the *C*-faucet. *C* stands for "cold" in English, but for "hot" in each of those languages (French *chaud*, Spanish, *caliente*, Italian *caldo*).

4 How To Use English

IN SOME CONTINENTAL EUROPEAN COUN-
tries, there are language academies which practically legislate the language. They tell people what is correct and
what is incorrect, set down rules for speaking and writing
the language, and crack down on anything that smacks of
a dialect or slang. Sometimes the people follow the dictates
of the academies, which are made up of learned scholars,
sometimes they don't. All languages change with the passing of time, and while the change can be slowed, it can
never be altogether halted.

Not that the academies really want to halt the process of
language change. They only want to turn it into what they
consider desirable channels. But the academy's view of
what is a desirable channel and the view of the great body
of speakers aren't always quite the same.

The speakers of English, both here and in Britain, have
never cared for a language academy. Instead, they prefer
to follow what they call "usage." But usage is a doubtful
guide. It cannot always be very accurately determined.
Two or more conflicting usages may go on at once, one
perhaps favored by the more educated, the other by those
who have not had much schooling. Many people say "It
is I"; others prefer "It is me"; some say "Whom did you
see?"; others "Who did you see?" Some pronounce *either*,
neither with the sound of *ee* in *see*, others with the sound of
i in *mine*.

"Usage" applies to many different things: sounds and
pronunciations, spelling, the meaning of words, the way

you use words in a sentence. Each of these items has its own background and history.

The sounds of English are pretty well fixed. There are, according to different views, twelve or thirteen vowel-sounds, nine or ten vowel-combinations, and, at the most, about thirty consonant-sounds or consonant-combinations. What usually happens when there is a local difference of pronunciation is that one of these sounds replaces another; but the sound that is replaced still exists in other words, so far as the person who makes the replacement is concerned. Let us say, for instance, that a Midwesterner says "father" with a good final -*r*, that you can hear, while a New Englander says "fathuh." Does this mean that the New Englander does not have the sound of *r* in his language? Not at all; both he and the Midwesterner will use the sound of *r* in a word like "read," and the New Englander may even use an *r* at the end of "idea" and pronounce it "idear." So the question of usage in sounds wears itself down to *local* usage, and since English speakers have more or less agreed that no locality shall have the upper hand in determining what is the proper pronunciation, usage is left somewhat up in the air. We can, of course, say that if the overwhelming majority of localities all agree in pronouncing a word a certain way, that is usage. But the usage of minorities is not altogether excluded. It is not quite the same thing as happens, say, in French, where the Academy says: "This is the proper pronunciation, and any other pronunciation is dialectal, incorrect, and inferior."

Now take the question of spelling. In some languages, like Spanish or Italian, the pronunciation determines the spelling. The written letters of the alphabet, or combinations of letters, indicate only one possible sound. This means that if you know how a word is pronounced, you don't have to learn how to spell it; you know in advance, because there is only one possible letter or letter-combination that can apply to that particular sound. But this is not at all true of English, where the sound of *f* may appear in writing as *f* ("fear"), or as *ph* ("Philadelphia"), or as *gh* ("enough"). In English also a spelling like *gh* may indicate an *f*-sound ("enough"), a *g*-sound ("ghost"), or be completely silent ("through"). The written letter *i* is differently pronounced in "I" and in "it," while the sound of *ee* in "see" may appear as *ee*, but also as *ie* ("siege"), *ei* ("receive"), *i* ("machine"), or half a dozen other ways. So we have to learn how to spell each word.

Why is all this? When English was Anglo-Saxon each sound was represented for the most part by one letter, and each letter of the alphabet had one sound. Then English pronunciation began to change. A word spelled *cniht* (and a little later *knight*) was pronounced at first *k-n-i-h-t;* then the speakers got tired of pronouncing a *k* in front of an *n* and an *h* in front of a *t;* they dropped both sounds, and at the same time drawled out the *i* (which at first had the sound of *i* in "it") until it got to have the sound of *i* in "mine." Now the word was pronounced *n-ī-t*, and it should have changed its spelling accordingly. But it didn't. People who don't mind changing their pronunciation feel that there is something sacred about writing, and that it shouldn't be disturbed. So they went on writing *cniht*, or *kniht*, or *knight*, when they were saying *n-ī-t*. Today they still spell "knight," though they haven't pronounced the word that way for nearly a thousand years. So our spelling in part reflects the pronunciation of centuries ago.

There was something else that came into play at the time when printing began. Before that, all writing was done by hand, and the people who wrote (they weren't many) spelled words pretty much as they pleased. The printers decided that it would be well to have some sort of regularity about the way words were spelled. But they found it hard to agree, and for centuries the spelling of some words fluctuated. The word we spell "music" was generally spelled "musick" until a little over a century ago. Back in the sixteenth century a word like "guest" might appear in print as "gest," "geste," "gueste," "ghest," "gheste." Even a simple word like "been" might appear as "bin" or "beene." It was not until recent times that people more or less agreed on how to spell words, and the agreement is still far from complete today (note that we spell "honor," "connection," but the British prefer "honour," "connexion"). Some people prefer "thru" to "through," "altho" to "although," even "nite" and "lite" to "night" and "light." Usage? Yes, but a very illogical and irregular usage.

Now take the meaning of words and the way they are used. In British usage, "corn" means any kind of food grain, especially wheat; in American usage, it means Indian corn, or maize. "Starve" means "to die of hunger" to most English speakers; but in English Yorkshire it means "to die of cold," or even "to be cold." "Contact" is generally used in expressions such as "to be in contact with"; but some people prefer to use it in this fashion: "to contact somebody." So usage in the matter of the meaning and use of words is not everything it might be. Here again, if we had a language academy, it would rule some meanings in and others out.

Last of all comes the way words are used in sentences. "I" and "me" are both fully legitimate and accepted words, but which of the two should be used after "it is," or after "between you and"? Everybody admits that "who" and "whom" both exist, but which one should be used before "did you see?"? Should you say "I lay on the bed" or "I laid on the bed"? "I seen him" or "I saw him"? "I shall go tomorrow" or "I will go tomorrow"? Considering the fact that you say "fields," "books," "pencils," etc., why not "sheeps," "oxes" and "deers"?

These are all points of grammar, and grammar may be defined as the code of usage for words and sentences. But grammar, like spelling, often lags behind speech. Furthermore, grammar is often based on the opinions of grammarians who are slightly out of touch with usage. But then again, what is usage? Plenty of people, including Churchill and Queen Elizabeth, say "It's me"; but plenty more say "It is I."

Maybe you don't care for this free and easy usage of English. Maybe you'd prefer a system where someone told you exactly what to say, and pronounced you right or wrong, without question or argument. But remember that English speakers have always been noted for their love of individual freedom. They resent having someone tell them what to do and order them about. It's a good way to be, even if it leads to a certain amount of uncertainty and argumentation.

Now if you go back over the examples we gave you above, you will notice that in some of them you are a little uncertain yourself, in others you are not. You may hesitate between "It is I" and "it is me," or "I shall" and "I will," but you will hardly hesitate between "oxes" and "oxen." There is the main point of usage. Usage, in order to be a real guide, has to be just about overwhelming. A bare majority of one or two votes does not make usage. Outside of very small children, practically no one says "oxes." You have never heard anyone say "Me went to the store," or "he saw I."

This means that it is perfectly possible to build up a grammar based on usage, provided in it we don't try to legislate on points where there is a decided difference of opinion among the speakers (these points, by the way, are not too numerous, and they can easily be set apart and presented as not yet settled). We can use that kind of a grammar, with the understanding that it is based on usage, that usage fluctuates and changes, that two or more usages may exist at one and the same time. When we are in doubt, we can let ourselves be guided by what we hear around us or, if we prefer, by what we see in writing, because writing represents a continued, traditional usage that is a little more lasting than what we hear in speech. As the language changes, we should change with it. But we need be in no hurry to hasten its change, or to seize every novelty and use it the minute it comes out.

What goes for grammar goes also for the pronunciation and meaning of words. There is no point to bucking the tide and setting yourself too far apart from the community you happen to be in. If everybody around you says "fig-ure," why insist on drawing attention to yourself by saying "figger"? If "corn" means what you eat off the cob to the people around you, why try to make it mean "wheat" to them? If the newspapers you read print "labor," "connection" and "defense," why not spell them that way yourself?

On the other hand, there is no particular reason to accept and use everything new that comes along, or to side invariably in your speech with the less educated and cultured elements of the community. It may be only a question of being known by the company you keep, but that, too, is important. If all or most of the people you have reason to look up to and try to imitate say "isn't" and "aren't" rather than "ain't," it is wise policy to follow their lead.

It is true that we have no language academy in America or Britain. But we do have a large body of educated people who set some sort of standard usage. They are normally engaged in intellectual callings, which means that they have more to do with the handling of language than other workers. They have more practice, more experience. They read more, they write more, they usually speak more. They know more words, and are more familiar with the art of putting them together. If you wanted to learn something about a car, you would try to get your information from a mechanic who knows the engine and the parts, rather than from someone who just drives occasionally. In the same way, you can better learn to handle the language from one who handles it all the time, or even professionally, than from one who uses it only occasionally and in only one way. Let the more educated sections of the community be your guide in matters of language, and let their usage be your usage. If you get nothing else from it, you will at least gain the reputation of being more educated, and that is worth while having when you seek employment or preferment.

At the same time, never look down upon anyone whose language does not come up to your own standards. He may have information of other kinds to place at your disposal. He may have lots of other fine qualities. His language, while it may not be the highest standard of today, may well lead to the standard language of tomorrow, as has so often happened in the past.

5 *How To Build Up Your English*

WHILE WE HAVE NO LANGUAGE ACADEMY for English, we do have something that partly serves the purpose, and that something is the dictionary. If you examine carefully one of the standard dictionaries, you will see that it gives quite a lot of information about words, their spelling, pronunciation, origin, meaning and uses. For spelling and pronunciation, don't be surprised if the dictionary gives you two or more choices. These double choices represent the various conflicting usages we have been talking about. If the dictionary is American, it will present current American usage first, but the British variant will also normally appear (for instance, *labor, labour;* or *fig'ûr, fig'ēr;* a dictionary printed in Britain would probably give *labour* and *fig'ēr* first). In cases where there are differences in American pronunciation itself, the first one given will usually be the more widely used (*tŏ-mā'-tō, tŏ-mä'-tō*). These double spellings and pronunciations are a notice to you to use your own judgment and make your own choice. It used to be that the pronunciation favored by the dictionaries was the New England variety, because that was where most of the dictionary makers came from; but that is no longer true.

Then the dictionary gives you the origin of the word, the language it first came from, whether it be Anglo-Saxon or Latin or French or Greek or whatever. Often the history of the word is traced, as where "belfry" is described as

119

coming from Old French *berfrei*, and then back to Germanic *berg-friede*, "guard the peace." Some dictionaries give you entrancing little word-histories, that give you an understanding of the meaning and use of the word such as you could never get otherwise. "Music," for instance, is described as going back through French and Latin to Greek *mousikē technē*, "musical technique," or "art of the Muses," any art presided over by the Muses, who were nine minor goddesses who according to the ancient Greeks had charge of song, poetry, art and science; notice how cut down is our modern meaning from the ancient.

In this connection, you may notice that for some words there is no given origin; this means that the word merely appeared in the language at a certain point of time, without any known or probable ancestor; it may have been a slang coinage of the Middle Ages at its outset, and the origin of most slang is obscure. If you use one of the larger dictionaries, however, it will tell you when and in what connection the word first appeared. Many words are described as coming from Middle English, which means the English spoken, roughly, from 1150 to 1550; but this is the same as saying that we don't know how they started or where they came from. Here again, the larger dictionaries will trace the word for you, as far back as it can be traced.

Next come the meanings and uses of the word. Some of these are archaic (which means antiquated, old-fashioned); some are dialectal; some are colloquial, vulgar or slang; some restricted to either British or American usage. If a word has a special meaning in one field of activity that differs from the general meaning, that is explained ("quarter," for example, has a dozen general meanings, several special nautical, military and mechanical meanings, and one very special meaning in heraldry).

All this means that we can get a great deal of guidance for our use of language out the dictionary. This means in turn that in our reading, or even in our speaking, we don't have to make blind stabs at pronunciations, meanings or spellings. We can find out. Some people get a lot of pleasure from just thumbing through a dictionary and learning about words at random. Others make it a practice to look up each and every word they come across about which they have any doubt whatsoever. They figure that knowledge is power, and they want to know.

A great deal of our information comes to us through speech, but there is a great deal more that comes to us in written form. When we read, we get, so to speak, an accumulation of knowledge out of the past. At the same time, we gain a firmer control over our use of the present-day language. People have been writing in English since the days of the Anglo-Saxons, and most of their writings have come down to us. By reading what they have written, we get a good view of the way the language has been and is being used, but that is far from all. We also get an insight into the customs and ways of English-speaking people in past centuries, how they lived, what they ate and drank, how they fought and played, what they thought. We find out how like ourselves they were, and yet how unlike. We can even trace the changes in their habits and customs and thinking, and the beginnings of our own. They had their problems, just as we have ours, and sometimes we can learn to solve ours from the way they solved theirs.

If we want to learn to speak and write well and effectively, there is no better way than to read what people have written in the past, for in their writings they pass on to us the accumulated experiences of the human race. Sometimes you hear people saying that we are living in a new era, in which everything is different from what it ever was. This is true only for what concerns mechanical inventions, and it isn't altogether true even there. But for human feelings, human problems, and human experience, the world has not changed too much. Human beings are still pretty much the same as they were in the days of Dickens, or Shakespeare, or Chaucer, or even Christ. It is interesting to read Roman history and find out that the great Roman Empire faced almost the same situations that our American nation faces today. The Romans made mistakes, and if we make the same mistakes it's largely because we won't bother to find out the ones they made and how they could have been avoided.

The time you spend in reading is never wasted. Reading, however, should be an intelligent, not a haphazard process. As you read, try to understand all that you are reading, not just a part of it. Try to get into the spirit and mood of the writer, and to follow his choice of words. Don't be satisfied with a general impression. Look up in the dictionary words you can't understand, and try to remember them, so you won't have to look them up a second time when you run across them again. Notice the way sentences are strung together to produce a pleasing effect on the ear. This happens especially in poetry, but it often occurs in ordinary prose as well. If you come across an author that you particularly like, try to imitate him in your own writing, using the words and combinations of words he uses. Since there will be more than one such author, after a time you will come out with a style of writing which, while it is a compromise or merger of all your favorites, will really be your own.

Watch your spelling when you write, and try to remember the way words are spelled in the dictionary, particularly the longer and harder words. If you get away from the accepted spelling, it isn't a tragedy, and great writers have done it before you. On the other hand, the tendency today is for the spelling of words to become more and more set, and people will think you are ignorant if you misspell too many words. The dictionary is always there for you to check up your spelling with.

Watch your pronunciation, and try to bring it in line with that of the people around you in whose command of the spoken language you have trust. Don't mumble, chew, or bite off your words. If a word seems too long to be comfortably handled, break it up into syllables, as the dictionary shows you how to do; pronounce each syllable separately, slowly at first, then faster; finally, bring your syllables together at normal speed. You will find that you are pronouncing the word clearly, easily and correctly.

As we said before, the English language is made up of sounds, of grammatical forms, of words with their meanings, and of the way the words are put together. The sounds you already possess. You also have the main grammatical forms (you know, for instance, that if you want to speak of one you say "book," "child," "foot," but if you want to speak of two or more you say "books," "children," "feet"). The field where you can really build up your language is in words and the way you combine them. The more words you know and can handle easily, the more power you have in your speech and writing, the two biggest ways you have of communicating with other people and influencing them. The dictionary is there to help you build up your word-hoard. English literature is there to show you how to use and combine those words so they will be most effective in obtaining the purpose you desire.

You can view both the dictionary and literature as tools. There are other tools you will use as time goes on, but these two are the most important, because they build up your speech and writing, and speech and writing can be used in any field you care to enter and in each one of your waking moments.

Watch your writing, and watch your speech. Keep them in the best state of repair you can. They both improve with use, so don't hesitate to use them. Add to both every time the opportunity arises.

PART FOUR

OTHER PEOPLE'S LANGUAGES

1 Hard and Easy Languages

IF ONE-TENTH OF THE WORLD'S POPULATION speaks English, then it is obvious that the other nine-tenths speak something else. What do they speak? One or another of the 2,795 languages which, side by side with English, exist on the present-day globe. To us, they are all foreign tongues.

If we acquire one or more of them, we shall have a means of communicating with the speakers of the one or ones we acquire, of finding out more about them than we ever could otherwise, of reading their literature as well as our own, and thereby adding the accumulated experiences of their group to those of our group.

This seems to be worth while. But at once questions begin to arise.

Which one of the 2,795 languages we don't know shall we begin with? How much of a job is it to learn a foreign tongue? Are they all equally hard, or are some easier than others?

We have already seen that out of the total number of languages spoken there are only thirteen that have fifty million or more speakers. It would seem wise to begin with one of these thirteen large, important world tongues, unless we have a special reason for starting with a minor one. What special reasons could there be? Suppose your parents planned to travel to Holland and spend some time there, it might be wise to take up Dutch, the language of

Holland, even though it is not one of the big thirteen. Or suppose one or both of your parents were born in Hungary, or Poland, or Sweden, and are in a position to train you in their native tongue, it might be very wise to start with Hungarian or Polish or Swedish, even though they are not among the thirteen giants.

Even if we restrict ourselves to the thirteen (really twelve, for English is one of the thirteen, and you already know English), we have quite a choice. Some of the twelve are likely to prove more useful than others. Hindustani and Bengali you would be likely to use only if you traveled to India; Malay would serve you only in Indonesia or Malaya, Japanese or Chinese only in Japan or China, Arabic in North Africa or southwest Asia. It is, of course, perfectly possible that you might have a very definite use for one of these languages, but from where you sit today it doesn't seem too likely.

On the other hand, if you go to Europe (and lots of Americans do these days), you are almost certain to run into French and German. If you go to Mexico, Central America, Cuba, Puerto Rico or South America, you are certain to run into Spanish, while in Brazil, the largest country in South America, you will find Portuguese. Russian is a language you may encounter, because at the present time the Soviet Union is the only real world rival of the United States. Italian is a language you will meet in southern Europe, and you will also encounter it on United States soil, because of the large number of Italians who have come here. This, by the way, is also true of Spanish, German and French.

Then there is another factor that has to be considered. Our own language and civilization have been built up on a background that is partly non-English. The languages that have contributed most to the modern English language are, as we have seen, Anglo-Saxon (of the same family and branch as German), Danish (another Germanic language, but of the Scandinavian branch), the French of the Normans, Latin and Greek, then, in lesser measure, Italian, Spanish and German. The cultures that have most influenced ours, after that of England, are the Classical (Latin and Greek), the Biblical (Hebrew and Greek), and those of medieval and Renaissance Europe (French, Italian, German, Spanish). The countries with which we enjoy the closest cultural and commercial relations today are those of western Europe (which means England, France, Italy, Germany, Spain), and those of the Western Hemisphere (in which English, Spanish and Portuguese are spoken). All in all, it seems that our high schools and colleges have not made any tremendous mistake in picking out as the languages to be studied by most American students Latin, French, Spanish and German, with additional provision made here and there for Italian, Greek, Hebrew, Portuguese and Russian.

Latin, Greek and Hebrew are valuable for their cultural, scientific and religious background, as well as for their contributions to English and to the western point of view. Among the modern languages, French, Spanish, German, Italian, Portuguese and Russian have all contributed in varying measure to our culture and language, and in addition have high practical importance in the world of today. We shall be safe in starting with any one of them, or any combination of two or three of them.

Let us not, however, forget those we fail to choose, but keep them in the background of our minds, with the hope of picking them up some day, or at least realize that they are there and what they stand for. And let us not forget, even if for the time being we neglect them, those other great languages of Asia and Africa, Chinese, Japanese, Hindustani, Malay, Arabic. Their speakers are advancing rapidly, and with the ease of modern travel and communications we may soon find ourselves in as close touch with them as we are today with the speakers of French and Spanish and German.

Is it hard to learn a foreign tongue? It all depends on what you mean by "learn," and on how you go about it. Knowing a language well means four things: that you are able to speak it so that people understand you; that you are able to understand what they say to you; that you are able to read what is written in it; that you are able to write in it so that your writing makes sense. You will notice that these four points apply to your own native English as well. Some people speak and understand fairly well, but they don't do much reading or writing. Others read a lot, but find it hard to make a speech. There is no such thing as being perfect in any language, including your own, so don't expect perfection in the language you are learning.

The best way to acquire a foreign language is to mingle with its speakers and talk to them and listen to them all the time, or as much time as you can. This is the way you learned to speak and understand English.

But you also had to learn to read and write English in school. Learning to read and write a language is best taught in the classroom. Speaking and understanding can be taught there, too, but of course you can't expect the amount of time you spend speaking in the classroom to equal that which you could spend on the outside.

Whichever way you go about it, don't be afraid of the foreign language. Remember, it's only a language. You proved you could learn a language when you learned English. Sail into the foreign language the same way. Open your mouth and speak. Of course you'll make mistakes. Who doesn't? You made mistakes when you started speaking English, too. But someone corrected you, and pretty soon you overcame the mistakes. You can do exactly the same thing in the foreign language. It may take time. It took time for you to learn English, too.

Are some foreign languages easier or harder than others? They really aren't if you start from scratch. This is proved by the fact that a French, or Russian, or Chinese boy or girl handles his or her language just about as well as you handle yours.

But when you start learning a foreign language at the age of twelve or thirteen, you're not starting from scratch. Your speaking habits are set. You have learned to produce well and easily about fifty of the hundreds of possible sounds you could produce, and it's an effort, at this stage, to learn to produce a new set. Also, you have now an established pattern of words, word-order, and meaning. It is natural for you to say "book" when you see a book, and not natural to say *livre*, or *kniga*, or *hon* (the French, Russian and Japanese ways of saying "book"). It is natural for you to say "I see him," and not natural to say "I him see," which is what you have to do if you're speaking French, or "him see-I," which is the Spanish or Italian way, with the "I" included in the "see." All this calls for a dislocation and rearrangement of your thought-and-word pattern.

But don't let this bewilder you. Suppose you are in the kitchen of your own home. You know where every pot and pan and dish is, and you could find what you want with your eyes shut. Then you go on a long visit to the home of a friend. You insist on helping with the dinner, and you go into his kitchen. He has pots and pans and dishes, too, but they are different from yours, and you don't know exactly where they are kept, or just how they are used. At first you have to inquire. Little by little, though, you get to know them. By the time you go back to your own home, you know all the locations and uses of two different sets of pots and pans and dishes in two different homes, and you don't get them confused. Anything wrong with that? You can even learn the kitchen arrangement of half a dozen homes if you have to. In the same way you can learn half a dozen different languages. Languages, after all, are tools, just like pots and pans and dishes.

Of course, the more your friend's kitchen is arranged like your own, the more easily you will learn. If he has pots and pans and dishes of sizes and shapes you've never seen before, you will have to inquire a little more closely into their use, and it will take you a little longer to learn.

Again, it's the same way with languages. The closer they are to your own, the easier they will seem to you. Which are the languages closest to English? English belongs to the great Indo-European family, so any language of that family should, generally, be easier than a non-member. But the family is divided into groups, and English belongs to the Germanic group. Hence a Germanic language, like German, Dutch or Danish, will come closer than, say, a Slavic language like Russian, or a tongue of India, like Hindustani. Actually, Dutch is about the closest of all, because the Anglo-Saxons and the ancestors of the present-day Hollanders stayed on together after the bonds with German and Scandinavian speakers had been cut. But don't forget that the Scandinavian-speaking Danes got in touch again with the Anglo-Saxons in the days of King Alfred, and poured many of their words into our language.

We have also seen, though, that the French-speaking Normans brought a great deal of French into English, and that much of our present-day language was and is brought in by scholars, writers and scientists from Latin and Greek. Latin was the direct ancestor not only of French, but also of Spanish, Italian and Portuguese. This means that Latin or any one of the Romance languages will show such strong links with English as to bring them practically on a par with the Germanic languages for what concerns ease of learning for an English speaker, and almost the same goes for Greek.

Here we come again to the languages most widely taught in American high schools and colleges—Latin, German, French, Spanish, Italian. They all belong to the number of languages that are most closely related to English, and are therefore easiest for us. If we take German, we shall find plenty of memory aids in the simple, everyday words of German. What can *Wasser* be but our own "water"? *Brot* is our "bread," *sehen* is our "see," *Gold* is our "gold." Just as we have "love, loved," but "see, saw," so the Germans have *liebe, liebte,* but *sehe, sah.*

If we take Latin, we will find *vir*, "man," from which our "virile" comes (what is "virile" but "manly"?); *femina* for "woman" (our "feminine"); *nauta* for "sailor" (our "nautical"); *milites* for "soldiers" (our "military" and "militia"); *agricola* for "farmer" (our "agriculture"); *decem* for "ten" (our "decimal"), and innumerable other words that are so closely linked with our English language that if we dropped from use all the words that come from Latin we would be practically unable to speak.

French, Spanish and Italian all have the selfsame words, and we will recognize each and every one of them. Our "general" comes from Latin *generalis;* the French is *général,* the Spanish *general*, the Italian *generale*; even the Germans took that Latin word, and use it as *General*. Often the words are a little disguised; but if you saw Latin *studium*, French *étude*, Spanish *estudio*, Italian *studio*, wouldn't you recognize it as English "study"?

In like manner, if you saw Greek *mikros* ("small") and *skopein* ("to look, see") wouldn't you think of "microscope," the instrument that enables you to see small things? And if you saw Greek *hippos* ("horse") and *dromos* ("road"), wouldn't you think of "hippodrome," a racecourse?

So don't be afraid of any of these languages. They are dear friends and close relatives of our own English. Like the pots and pans and dishes in your friend's kitchen, their words and the way they are arranged may differ in size or use from your own, but they are still tools you can learn to use. Whichever one (or ones) you start with, look it squarely in the eye, seize it firmly by the hand, and start using it at once. Never mind if you make mistakes at first. Everybody makes mistakes. Soon you'll learn to correct your mistakes, and you'll find that each new language you become acquainted with is like a new friend, who takes you into his home, shows you around, and tells you to act as though you were one of the family.

2 Languages of the Western Hemisphere

IN UNDERTAKING A GEOGRAPHICAL SURVEY of the world's languages, it would seem natural to start with our own neighborhood. The Western Hemisphere, where we live, has more wide open spaces and fewer people than the Old World. Strangely, however, it has more languages.

When we think of Western Hemisphere languages, our mind runs, first and foremost, to our own English, which holds sway in the United States, Canada and Alaska; then to the Spanish of most of the lands south of the Rio Grande; perhaps also to the Portuguese of Brazil and the French of eastern Canada, Haiti, and French possessions in the Caribbean, like the island of Martinique, and in South America, like French Guiana. If we are really keen on our language geography, we may also think of the Dutch of Dutch Guiana and the Danish of Greenland, also spoken in the Virgin Islands before Denmark turned them over to us.

These languages, English, Spanish, Portuguese, French, Dutch and Danish, along with the tongues of millions of immigrants to the Western Hemisphere, notably German and Italian, are indeed large and important languages, but they belong to the Western Hemisphere only by adoption, since they all originated in Europe. It is true that there are over three times as many English speakers, Spanish speakers and Portuguese speakers in North, Central and South America as there are in Europe, but the fact remains that

English started in England, Spanish in Spain, Portuguese in Portugal. French, Dutch and Danish never got in the Western Hemisphere anything like the foothold that the other three did, and the absolute majority of their speakers are still on their European home soils.

The truly native languages of the Western Hemisphere are the languages of the Eskimos, Aleuts and American Indians, and these are so numerous as to constitute almost half of all the tongues of the earth. This is surprising, since most of them have few speakers—a few hundred, or a few thousand.

The American Indian languages present some of the most absorbing puzzles of the language world. Are they really native to American soil, or did they come, as their speakers are supposed to have come, from northeastern Asia across Bering Strait? Are they really separate languages, or are they just dialects of a much smaller number of big languages, or perhaps of one single big language? Are they in any way linked with any of the languages of the Old World, particularly those of Siberia? The experts who have compared the two sets of languages don't seem inclined to believe it, and yet shouldn't there be such a link if the American Indians came from Asia?

There is no sure answer to any of these questions. Until the coming of the white man, American Indian languages were for the most part unwritten, and a language that is not written is at a terrific disadvantage. For one thing, it has no records outside of what is handed down by word of mouth; this means that we can't trace it back through the centuries to its earlier forms, study it throughout its history, and discover links that may have disappeared later with other languages in their earlier form. Secondly, an unwritten language changes much faster than one that has a written form, because the written language acts as a brake upon the spoken language and gives the speakers some sort of check on the "mistakes" they may be making and a chance to "correct" themselves by bringing themselves back in line with the forms sanctified by tradition.

It is not quite true that all American Indian languages were unwritten. The Mayas of Central America and the Aztecs of Mexico had a system of writing on stone that reminds us of the ancient Egyptian hieroglyphics. But the key to their writing has not been surely established, and at all events it seems to have been the kind of writing that stands for ideas rather than spoken sounds, which would be of no help in preserving spoken language forms. The Incas of Peru had an ingenious system of *quipus*, or knotted ropes, by means of which they could send limited messages at a distance, but this is only a symbolic language. The North American Indians often left records of their doings on bark, but these were pictures, not a true written language.

There is no point to enumerating the languages of the Indians of North, Central and South America, which are well over one thousand in number. Many of them have been grouped together into families, like the Algonquian or the Iroquoian, but when you try to connect up these families you seem to get nowhere, for they are as different from one another as English, Turkish and Chinese. Of course, it is possible that the link was there once, and that in the course of time and countless wanderings it was lost. The same may be said of the possibility of a link with the tongues of Siberia.

Fenimore Cooper and the Westerns have made us familiar with the names of a great many American Indian languages of the United States, which generally coincide with the names of tribes—Shoshone and Cheyenne and Sioux and Apache and Arapahoe. Today the speakers of American Indian languages on United States soil are comparatively few—less than half a million. Yet some of their languages are curiously alive. In Brooklyn, there is a church where the services are carried on in Mohawk, one of the Iroquois dialects, for the benefit of several dozen Mohawk Indians who live in the neighborhood. In the Southwest, Navajo is still a spoken tongue, and Navajo speakers were used by the Army during the last war to send and receive radio messages that would not be understood by the enemy.

In Canada, numerous Indian languages appear, many of them crossing the border into the United States. In Alaska, Eskimo and Aleut languages are spoken, while other Eskimo dialects appear in Greenland. Mexico has numerous American Indian languages, including the Nahuatl of the Aztecs, which is definitely related to the Ute of the western U. S., and it is estimated that about one-tenth of Mexico's population, or close to two million people, still speak nothing but Indian tongues, supplemented perhaps by a few Spanish words and phrases. The same situation holds in the Republics of Central America, notably Guatemala, where the ancient civilization of the Mayas lives on in their spoken language.

Arawak and Carib languages appear on the islands of the Caribbean, while South America is a happy hunting ground for researchers in American Indian tongues, which are very much alive and in use in practically all South American countries. In Paraguay, while Spanish is the official language, the majority of the population goes on speaking Tupi-Guaraní. But the most widespread of the South American Indian languages is Quechua, which extends from Ecuador, through Bolivia and Peru, down to northern Argentina. It is estimated that at least four million people still speak Quechua.

Until the beginning of the twentieth century, the American Indian languages were generally neglected, and many of them died out with their speakers. Since 1900 or thereabouts, there has been a quickening of interest in these tongues, some of which had already been recorded by missionaries, and a whole generation of anthropologists and linguists has been devoting painstaking study to them, with the result that they have become far better known. Their study has cast a good deal of light on the nature of spoken language in general. Their structures, that is to say, the way they put words together to express ideas and meanings, have been found to be so widely different both from one another and from the better-known languages of Europe, Asia and Africa, that many old beliefs about language have been completely exploded.

From the practical standpoint, however, the importance of the American Indian languages is limited. It is just barely conceivable that you might find yourself in a remote village in Mexico or Peru where Spanish would not serve you, and you would have to resort to Nahuatl or Quechua.

The Western Hemisphere languages of practical importance and wide range are English, Spanish and Portuguese, followed at some distance by French. English, as we have seen, is a Germanic language of the Indo-European family with a large mixture of Latin-Romance. Spanish, Portuguese and French are Romance tongues directly derived from Latin. The number of people you can reach with English in the Western Hemisphere comes close to two hundred million, located mostly in the United States and Canada, but with a liberal sprinkling elsewhere.

Spanish is the official tongue of one North American country (Mexico), two island republics (Cuba, Santo Domingo), one U. S. island possession (Puerto Rico), six Central American republics (Guatemala, Costa Rica, Honduras, Nicaragua, Salvador, Panama), and nine South American countries (Venezuela, Colombia, Ecuador, Bolivia, Peru, Paraguay, Uruguay, Argentina, Chile). The total population of this Spanish-speaking world is close to a hundred million, and the countries it includes are lands with which we enjoy friendly relations and carry on a large and growing commerce, so Spanish is an extremely important language for us. It is a fairly easy language, too. We shall tell you more about it when we come to Europe, the continent where it originated.

Portuguese is the language of a single South American country, Brazil, but that country is the largest one in South America, with an area larger than that of the United States and a population of nearly sixty million, which is constantly growing. Brazil is among our most loyal and trusted friends and allies, and it is the country from which we get most of our coffee and a good deal of our rubber. The Portuguese language came to Brazil with Portuguese settlers, who occupied the country in much the same way that the English settlers occupied what is now our eastern seaboard. Portuguese is a language that is very close to Spanish, and yet different.

The French of Haiti, eastern Canada and the French Western Hemisphere possessions is a third Romance language, of the same stock as Spanish and Portuguese. But while the majority of Spanish and Portuguese speakers are located in the Western Hemisphere with us, the French speakers of the Western Hemisphere are only a minority of the total number of French speakers. Still, they number close to ten million, and the fact that French far outstrips Spanish and Portuguese on the European continent and elsewhere throughout the world makes it one of the most important languages for us to consider.

It is worth while at this point to mention two other European languages which, while they are not official, national languages anywhere in the Western Hemisphere, have sent over here such large numbers of their speakers that they can be heard almost anywhere in North or South America. These languages are Italian and German. At least ten million speakers of each of these two important European tongues have settled on our side of the Atlantic, with the heaviest concentrations in the United States, Argentina, Brazil, Uruguay and Chile. Italian is a fourth member of the Romance group, closely linked to Spanish, Portuguese and French, while German is, like English, a Germanic tongue.

Nor should we forget that large numbers of Western-Hemisphere Spanish and French speakers have crossed land and water boundaries into United States soil. Many Spanish speakers are to be found in our southwestern States, especially Texas, New Mexico, Arizona and California, while other Spanish speakers from Puerto Rico have settled recently in large numbers in New York City. French speakers from eastern Canada have come down into our New England States, especially Rhode Island and Massachusetts. We even have groups of Portuguese speakers, largely from the Azores, on the Massachusetts seacoast and in California.

All these languages, and many more, are readily available to us, particularly if we live in the areas where large foreign-speaking groups have settled. In a city like New York, it is the easiest thing in the world to tune in on any one of dozens of foreign-language programs on the radio, and you can attend foreign-language movies in French, Spanish, German, Italian, Russian, Swedish and even Chinese and Japanese.

One of the easiest and most pleasant ways to learn a foreign tongue is to make friends with a boy or girl who speaks one, and trade conversations with him. He is usually eager to improve his English, and you can make a deal with him: "Tell me how to say things in your language, and I'll tell you how to say them in mine." You can also have pen-pals in foreign countries. They will write you in their language, correct the letters you send them, tell you all about their countries and how they live, if you return the compliment in English. Then, if you ever get to travel to their country, you will find ready-made friends who will show you around. And if they come here, you can show them the sights, and at the same time proudly show off your foreign connections to your neighborhood friends.

3 The Languages of Europe

EUROPE IS NOT SO IMPORTANT NOW AS IT was in the eighteenth and nineteenth centuries, when world civilization revolved almost completely around it, with North and South America playing the role of cultural outposts or satellites, and Asia and Africa largely acting the part of colonial domains.

But Europe still holds a most important world post. For one thing, it is the cradle of this western culture of which we are so proud, and still supplies a great deal of our music, art and literature. For another, it holds a total population of well over five hundred million—at least one-fifth of the earth's total, and almost double that of the Western Hemisphere. Thirdly, it has a productive, commercial and scientific capacity that in many fields outstrips our own.

The languages of Europe are not so numerous as those of the American Indians, the African Negroes, or the Asiatics. There are only about thirty whose names are generally known. But in return, they are for the most part important languages, with large speaking populations, a long and well-known history, and profound cultural achievements. Of the world's thirteen languages that have over fifty million speakers, seven were born on European soil (English, French, Spanish, Italian, Portuguese, German, Russian). The three leading tongues of the Western Hemisphere (English, Spanish and Portuguese) are all European in origin.

143

For what concerns family ties, practically all the tongues of Europe are related, and belong to the great Indo-European family. But they do not all belong to the same branch. Several among them are Germanic (English, German, Dutch, the Scandinavian tongues). Others are Romance (French, Spanish, Italian, Portuguese, Rumanian). Still others are Slavic (Russian, Polish, Czech, Serbo-Croatian, Bulgarian). Some, like Greek and Albanian, are minor, separate branches of the Indo-European family. A few are Celtic (Irish, Welsh, Breton). Lithuanian and Latvian, or Lettish, are Baltic tongues, closer to the Slavic than to any of the other branches, but not close enough to be merged with Russian and Polish.

What European languages do not belong to the family? In the north of Europe, lying between Sweden and Russia, is Finland. The four or five million Finns, along with the Lapps of the Arctic Circle and the Estonians of the Baltic coast, speak tongues of another language family, the Uralic. Then, in the very heart of Europe, is another Uralic tongue, Hungarian. These Uralic tongues, as their name implies, came originally from the region of the Ural Mountains, which separate Europe from Asia. Astride the Bosporus is another Asiatic language, Turkish, whose relatives stretch all the way across northern Asia to Mongolia and Manchuria, and are called Altaic, after the Altai Mountains of central Asia. Turks, Tatars, Mongols and Manchus were in the past great invaders and conquerors (think of Genghis Khan, Tamerlane, the Turkish conquest of Constantinople, and the Manchu conquest of China), but today their number is small, and they have turned to peaceful pursuits.

Finnish, Hungarian and Turkish may therefore be said to form three Asiatic spearheads driven into Europe at widely different points. A good many linguists are con-

THE LANGUAGES OF EUROPE

vinced that there is a link between Uralic and Altaic languages, while others have been trying to prove a connection between Ural-Altaic on the one hand and Indo-European on the other.

One more language, a very mysterious one, falls outside the Indo-European family. This is Basque, the tongue of a little over one million people who live in the Pyrenees, along the Bay of Biscay, astride the French-Spanish border. Their language has no connection with French, Spanish, or any other European tongue, and there are many people who believe that it is the only survivor of a much larger family of languages that existed in Europe before the coming of Indo-European speakers. It is a difficult language, and the Basques circulate the legend that at one time the devil tried to learn their tongue, so that he might tempt its speakers, but gave up in disgust when, after seven years of study, he discovered that all he had learned to say was "yes" and "no."

English is, of course, the language of Great Britain and Northern Ireland, and it is also spoken by nearly all the inhabitants of Eire, the Irish Free State. This means that a little over fifty million people in the British Isles speak English, in its British variety, as their mother-tongue. But in addition to the various British dialects that we have mentioned elsewhere, there are other languages spoken in the British Isles. There is Irish, a Celtic tongue which the government of Eire has been trying hard to bring back into general use among Eire's three million inhabitants. But it is handicapped by the fact that almost all Irishmen already speak English, and English is a great world language which serves you almost everywhere you may go, while Irish is not. Irish is a beautiful but strange-sounding language, and its writing is strange, too, coming down as it

does from a form of handwriting that was used by the
monks in the Middle Ages. A very close relative of Irish is
Scots Gaelic, spoken by less than 100,000 Scottish High-
landers, and a third member of the Celtic family is Welsh,
used by about one million people in Wales, the western
part of the island of Britain. Another Celtic language,
Cornish, used to be spoken in Cornwall, the peninsula that
juts off the southwestern extremity of Britain, but its speakers have died away, and their descendants use English.

On the European continent, foreign languages begin in
earnest. France, a nation of some forty-five million, speaks
French, which is also used in southern Belgium and western
Switzerland, bringing the total number of native French
speakers on European soil to well over fifty million. But
this does not exhaust the possibilities of French in Europe,
because even outside the three countries named, French is
widely spoken by educated people all over the continent;
in countries like Italy, Spain, Portugal and Holland, millions of cultured natives speak French fluently; one often
encounters Russians and Poles who know no English, but
who know French.

On the other hand, there are corners in France where a
different language is spoken, even though its speakers also
know French. The physical appearance of France on a
map has often been likened to a coffee-pot. The spout of
the pot, which juts out into the Atlantic, is called Brittany,
and was so named because it was settled by Britons fleeing
the Anglo-Saxons who had invaded Britain. These British
refugees brought with them their Celtic language, which
turned into present-day Breton. Since they were exactly
the same people as the Welsh, who solved the problem of
getting away from the Anglo-Saxons by withdrawing to
the west into the mountains of Wales, it is not surprising

that Breton should be quite close to Welsh—so much so that it is claimed the fishermen from the two countries, when they meet out in the Atlantic, can still carry on a conversation. The speakers of Breton are over one million, but they practically all speak French, too.

In the southwestern corner of France there are Basque speakers, while at the other end of the Pyrenees, on the Mediterranean side, are speakers of Catalan, a Romance tongue that differs from both Spanish and French, and that, like Basque, spills over the Pyrenees, with most of its speakers on the Spanish side. There are German and Italian minorities along the German and Italian borders of France. But French, like English, is a language that is easily picked up, and there are very few people living on French soil who do not speak it, along with their native Breton, Basque, Catalan, German or Italian.

French is a Romance tongue, which means that it stems largely from Latin, the tongue of the Romans who conquered and colonized Gaul, as the country was called in ancient times. The Romans intermingled with the Celtic-speaking population, which soon dropped Celtic and took to speaking Latin. In the course of centuries, the Latin of the Gallo-Romans developed into present-day French, just as Anglo-Saxon developed into English. We have seen that the transformation of English was aided by the French-speaking Normans, and the transformation of Latin into French was similarly aided by the Franks, a Germanic tribe that came into Gaul around A.D. 500 and merged with the Latin-speaking population. The Franks eventually gave their own name to the country, but they dropped their Germanic tongue in favor of Latin, just as the Normans dropped their French in favor of English. But just as the Normans put many French words into English, so the

Franks put many Germanic words into the Latin of Gaul as it turned into French.

The French language of today is well worth learning, because it can be used, like English, almost anywhere. The United Nations have five official languages (English, French, Spanish, Russian, Chinese), but the two most frequently used are English and French.

Good spoken French is a delight to the ear, but it calls for several sounds that don't exist in English. Some French vowel-sounds require the thrusting out of the lips (French *u*, for instance, calls for putting your lips into position for the *oo* of *food*, and then, without drawing them back, trying to pronounce the *ee* of *meet*). Other French vowel-sounds call for shutting off the passage between your nose and your throat (you can do it perfectly by holding your nose, but that isn't necessary), and pronouncing the vowel with your nose closed off.

If we cross the Pyrenees we come into Spain, the birthplace of the Spanish language which is so widespread in our Western Hemisphere. There are less than twenty-five million Spanish speakers in Spain, as against nearly one hundred million on our side of the Atlantic.

In Spain, as in France, there are linguistic minority groups, most of whom speak the official Spanish along with their own languages. The three chief linguistic minorities of Spain are the Basques in the northeast, the Catalans along the Mediterranean coast, particularly around the city of Barcelona and in the Balearic Islands, and the Galicians in the northwestern corner of the country, right above Portugal. Galician is really a form of Portuguese, which is the main tongue of the western part of the Iberian Peninsula. Here again we have a repetition of what happens with Spanish; there are little more than eight million Portuguese speakers in Portugal, but over fifty million in Brazil.

Spanish and Portuguese are both Romance languages, coming down straight from Latin. In both, however, there are numerous words from ancient Iberian, modern Basque, and Arabic. The last are particularly numerous, because the Arabic-speaking Moors overran all of Spain and Portugal except the extreme northern strip in the eighth century A.D., and they were not driven back across the Strait of Gibraltar until 1492, the very same year that America was discovered. During the six centuries or more of Moorish rule in central and southern Spain and Portugal, words like "algebra," "alcohol" and "alkali" (note that they start with *al-*, which is Arabic for "the") came into the Spanish and Portuguese languages, which then spread them on to the other languages of Europe, including English. But don't think every word with *al-* is Arabic. If you travel to Spain, you may have a chance to visit the Alcázar of Toledo, a lovely Moorish palace. *Alcázar* looks like a very Arabic word, but is really the Latin *castrum*, "military camp," to which the Moors prefixed their article *al-*. *Castrum* had a diminutive form, *castellum*, "small fortified camp," from which we get "castle." In French, *castellum* became *chastel*, then *château*, a word we have borrowed. So you see that "castle," "château" and "Alcázar" are one and the same word.

Spanish is a language of clear, easy sounds, with a fairly simple grammar, and a vocabulary that has many connections with our own. It also has extremely simple writing rules, many of which were definitely designed to be of help to the learner. For instance, if you have a question in Spanish, you not only have a question mark at the end, but also an upside down question mark at the beginning, to warn you that a question is coming, so that you may give it the proper tone of the voice. "How much is this book?" appears in written Spanish as *"¿Cuánto cuesta este libro?"* Notice also that *cuánto*, "how much" is connected with our "quantity," *cuesta* with our "cost," *libro* with our "library." The Portuguese is almost the same: *"Quanto custa êste livro?"*

For that matter, so is the Italian: *"Quanto costa questo libro?"* Italian is the native tongue of nearly fifty million people in Italy, the southern part of Switzerland, the extreme southeastern corner of France, the islands of Sicily, Sardinia and Corsica (Corsica, Napoleon's birthplace, belongs to France, but the native Corsican speech is an Italian, not a French dialect). In return, there are small groups of French, German and Slavic speakers in the northern provinces of Italy, along the Alps. Italian is also widely spoken along the eastern Adriatic coast, in Yugoslavia, and in various parts of Africa that were once Italian colonies. You can hear Italian currently spoken in many cities of the United States and South America.

Italian is the most direct descendant of Latin, which is quite natural, since Latin was originally spoken in central Italy, around the city of Rome, which is now Italy's capital. It is still possible today to construct a sentence that is perfectly good Latin and perfectly good Italian at the same time. Italian is a lovely-sounding, sonorous language of clear vowels and consonants, particularly well adapted for singing (most of our operas are sung in Italian). It is also the language of the fine arts, which during the Middle Ages and Renaissance flourished on Italian soil, especially in the cities of central and northern Italy, Florence and Siena and Bologna and Venice.

But Italian is also a language of many and widely different dialects, some of which sound so unlike the national tongue as to be practically different languages. This can prove embarrassing if you learn standard Italian and then come up against someone who speaks only the Neapolitan, or Sicilian, or Lombard dialect. Fortunately, today most Italians learn the standard language in the schools, and can use it.

Switzerland might be described as the meeting-ground of the Romance and the Germanic languages. In the south of Switzerland the people speak Italian or Rumansh, a Romance variety that is a sort of cross between Italian and French. In western Switzerland, around Geneva and Lausanne, they speak French. In central, northern and eastern Switzerland, around Zürich, Berne and Lucerne, the official language is German, and the popular language is a German dialect, which the Swiss call *Schwyzer-Tütsch*, or "Swiss German." All four languages, German, French, Italian and Rumansh, are officially recognized in Switzerland, but don't get the idea that all the Swiss speak all four of them.

German is the great passkey to central Europe, and the most widespread language spoken on European soil. English and Spanish outstrip it, but only because they are so widely used in the Western Hemisphere. Russian outstrips it, but only because it is used in Asia as well as in Europe. About one hundred million Europeans speak German. They include the inhabitants of Germany, of Austria and of most of Switzerland, in all of which countries German is the official, national language. They also include millions of Czechs, Poles, Hungarians, Yugoslavs, Hollanders, Swedes and Danes. The reasons why German is widespread in all these countries are various. Czechoslovakia, Hungary, and large parts of Yugoslavia and Poland used to form part of the Austro-Hungarian Empire before the first World War, which broke out in 1914. The chief official language of that Empire was German, and most of the people who

OTHER PEOPLE'S LANGUAGES 153

lived in the Empire found it convenient to learn German, whatever might be their own mother-tongue. The Empire broke up at the end of the war, but the great German tradition remained. In the case of countries like Holland, Sweden and Denmark, it was more a case of being close neighbors to Germany and constantly trading with the big country of central Europe.

German is, like English and Dutch, a West Germanic language, which makes it very close to us. But official, literary German is based largely on the High German dialects of the mountains rather than on the Low German dialects of the seacoast, to which Anglo-Saxon originally belonged. This makes English closer to Dutch, or to the German dialects of seacoast cities like Hamburg or Bremen, than to the standard German language. The big split between High and Low German came somewhere between the fifth and the ninth centuries A.D., and affected mainly certain consonant-sounds. Where all the Germanic languages had a *d* before the split, High German shifted to a *t* (English "bread," "dance," German *Brot, Tanz*); where they all had a *p*, High German shifted to a *pf* or *f* (English "pepper," German *Pfeffer*); where they had a *t*, High German shifted for the most part to *ss* (English "water," "foot," German *Wasser, Fuss*).

Dutch, which was like Anglo-Saxon a Low German dialect, did not make the shift, and so Dutch has usually the same consonants as English (*water* for "water," *voet* for "foot," pronounced almost as in English). Dutch is the language of Holland, a country of about ten million people, and a variety of Dutch called Flemish is used by over half the population of Belgium (the other half speaks French). About two million South Africans, descendants of the Dutch Boers, speak Afrikaans, which is derived from

Dutch. Dutch is also widely spoken in Dutch possessions and former possessions, like Indonesia, so that Dutch, Flemish and Afrikaans together come very close to the twenty million mark.

Other Germanic languages of the Scandinavian branch are Swedish (about eight million), Norwegian (three million), Danish (four million) and Icelandic (about 150,000). These languages, as we have seen, have contributed rather heavily to English. From them we have gotten such common words as "they," "them," "are," "ill," "cut," "knife," "sister." They are quite close to one another, and the speaker of one of them can usually understand most of what is said by the speaker of another. Icelandic, however, has remained "frozen" just about where it was at the time of the Vikings, so that while the grammar of Danish or Norwegian resembles that of modern English, the grammar of Icelandic reminds one of the grammar of Anglo-Saxon.

As you travel eastward in Europe, you begin to touch the lands where Slavic languages are spoken—Polish in Poland (about twenty-five million), Czech and Slovak in Czechoslovakia (close to fifteen million), Serbo-Croatian and Slovenian in Yugoslavia (over fifteen million), Bulgarian in Bulgaria (about eight million). But the big language of this family is the Russian of the Soviet Union, spoken by well over one hundred million people in eastern Europe and northern Asia. There are two other Soviet languages that are closely allied to Russian; they are Ukrainian, spoken in the southern part of European Russia by about forty-five million people, and White Russian, near the Polish border, with nearly ten million. The total population of the Soviet Union is estimated at about 220 million, and of these at least three-fourths have Russian, Ukrainian or White Russian as their mother-tongue. The others speak about 140 assorted languages, but they are small and little known. Many of them are of Uralic or Altaic stock, and therefore related to the Finnish, Hungarian and Turkish of Europe. There is reason to believe that most of these speakers of minor Soviet languages have by this time learned Russian, which is the official, or "binding" language of the Soviets.

Russian is a language of sounds which to us are strange, but not too difficult. The grammar of Russian may at first seem complicated, but that is only because it has, like Icelandic, remained closer to the original Indo-European state of affairs than has English. There is considerable similarity between Russian grammar and the grammar of the old Classical languages, Latin and Greek.

The Russians write in an alphabet called Cyrillic, which is mostly drawn, like the Roman alphabet we use, from the ancient Greek alphabet. It, too, looks strange at first, but it is not too difficult to master. Cyrillic alphabets are used also by Ukrainian, White Russian, Serbian and Bulgarian, but Polish, Czech, Slovak, Croatian and Slovenian use Roman characters.

The Slavic languages are close to one another, and a good many of their words are old Indo-European roots that we use as well. Our "nose," for example, is *nos* in all the main Slavic languages (it is *Nase* in German, *nasus* in Latin, *naso* in Italian, *nez* in French, proving that everybody had a nose when they were all speaking Indo-European, and that the name stuck to the nose). But some of the Slavic words, while connected with ours, are curiously disguised, and you have to be a language detective to figure out the link. Take, for instance, the Russian word for "bread" (*khleb* in writing, but usually pronounced *hlyep*). You would say at first glance that it cannot possibly be connected with any English word. But now remember that our "loaf" was *hlaif* in Old Germanic (we didn't like the sound of an *h* before an *l*, and dropped it, but the Russians didn't mind it, and kept it). Then, when we recall that an Indo-European *p* was shifted to *f* in the Germanic languages (our English "foot" corresponds to Latin *ped-*, Greek *pod-*), you can see that before the shift from *p* to *f* took place, the Germanic form was *hlaip*, which is not very different from *hlyep*. If anybody is to be blamed for the big difference between "loaf" and *khleb* today, it is we rather than the Russians. We are the ones who moved away.

We have mentioned Greek very often in these pages. Greek was one of the great languages of ancient times, but it is also the modern spoken tongue of Greece, a country of about eight million. Modern spoken Greek has changed somewhat from the ancient Greek of Homer and Plato, but in written form it is still quite close. In modern Greek you will find words that we use as well. *Ge* is "earth" and *grapho* is "I write," and there you have "geography." *Arithmo* means "I count," and it gives you "arithmetic." *Bios* is "life," *logos* is "word," and the two together give us "biology." *Strategos* is "general," and it gives us "strategy." The Greek alphabet, which gave rise to the Roman that we use, is still used by the modern Greeks. We should not have any trouble with it, considering that all the letters of the Greek alphabet are used by our college fraternities and sororities.

In the eastern part of the Balkan Peninsula we find the last large Romance language, with about fifteen million speakers, Rumanian. Rumanian is the descendant of the Latin spoken by the Roman soldiers who conquered the old Roman province of Dacia around A.D. 100. But in the fifth century, Dacia, or Rumania, was cut off from the rest of the Roman world by waves of invading barbarians who occupied the territory in between. So Rumanian is a Romance language that grew up all by itself. It has plenty of Slavic, Turkish and Greek words, but its structure and vocabulary are basically Latin, a fact of which the Rumanians are very proud.

Two other European languages may be mentioned, each of which forms a separate Indo-European branch, although the speakers of one are only about one million, and those of the other do not run over two or three million. They are Albanian, spoken in the western Balkans, and Armenian, spoken in the Caucasus Mountains, between Asiatic Turkey and European Russia.

One interesting fact may be called to mind in connection with the languages of Europe. We have seen one country, Belgium, where two languages, French and Flemish, are officially used side by side, with many Belgians speaking both. In Switzerland, we have seen four official tongues, German, French, Italian and Rumansh, and while all Swiss do not speak all four, a good many Swiss speak at least two. In France, there are people who speak French, and also Breton, or Basque, or Catalan, or Italian, or German. In Britain, there are people who speak English and also Welsh or Scots Gaelic. We might add that along practically every European border line there are plenty of people who speak fluently the languages on both sides of the border. This ability to speak two languages well is known as bilingualism (it can even be trilingualism, or plurilingualism). The fact that there are in Europe so many people who are bilingual or trilingual or plurilingual should make us pause and think. It proves that it isn't so difficult to learn one or two or three additional languages, and each language we learn is an additional string to our bow.

4 The Languages of Asia, Africa and Oceania

ASIA IS THE CONTINENT THAT CONTAINS the greatest population of all—well over one billion, or about half the earth's total. Accordingly, it is not surprising that in Asia we find the widest diversity of languages.

The northern part of the continent is occupied by the Soviet Union, and here the main languages, outside of Russian, are of the same family as Turkish, Finnish and Hungarian. But the population of Siberia and Mongolia is small for the vast extent of territory. The big population centers are farther south, in China, India and Japan.

First in numbers and importance among the languages of Asia is Chinese, with something close to half a billion speakers. Of course they don't all speak alike. The dialects that are so numerous and varied in our western languages are even more numerous and varied in China. A man from Peking in the northeast, one from Canton in the south, one from Shanghai on the eastern coast, and one from Chung King, in the western interior, cannot understand one another if each uses his own dialect. But the Chinese have one great advantage, a common written language. Since their writing is based on portraying ideas, not sounds, it works independently of the spoken word, somewhat like the numeral system that we have in common with the Russians, the Germans, the French. If I write the figure 8, it will be understood by all to mean "eight," though the Russian will pronounce it "*vosyem,*" the German "*acht*" and the Frenchman "*huit.*" In like manner, the Chinese written character for "man" will be pronounced *jên, nyin, yên* and in many other different ways by the inhabitants of various localities in China, but all will understand its meaning.

However different they may be, the spoken dialects of China, and those of several other languages of southeastern Asia (Siamese, or Thai, Burmese, Tibetan, some languages of French Indo-China) have many characteristics in common. They all consist of words of only one syllable. Many of these one-syllable words can be run together, in the same fashion that we run together "rail" and "road" and get "railroad." But you could not have in these languages words like "language," or "spoken," or "different." Nor could you have any endings on these words, as when we tack -*ing* on to *write* and get "writing," or even -*s* on to *dog* and get "dogs." Nor can we take a word like "I" and change it into "me." Chinese shows the full meaning of words, and their connection with other words in the sentence, only by the way the words are strung together. "I shall write" works out something like this: "I bright day write" ("bright day" is the optimistic Chinese way of saying "tomorrow"). "I see him," "he sees me" run: "I see he," "he see I." A sentence like "How are you?" runs *ni hao pu hao,* which actually means "You good not good" ("Are you well, or aren't you?").

Chinese and its kindred languages have something our languages do not have, or rather, we use it for a different purpose. In English, we can pronounce a name like "George" in different ways: if we say "George did it," the word "George" will sound straight and flat. If we answer a knock on the door, we will say "George?" with a questioning upswing of the voice. If we are blaming George for something, we will say "George, how could you?", and our voice will fall as we pronounce the name. If we are calling George from a distance, cupping our hands, our voice is apt to fall, then rise:- "Geo-orge!" Chinese uses these tones of the voice (some languages and dialects of this family use far more than four) to indicate entirely different meanings for what would otherwise be the same word. There is a word *ma*, which according to the tone in which it is pronounced can mean "horse," "mother," "flax," or act as a spoken question mark.

How do the Chinese, Siamese and others who speak these languages remember their tones? It is no trick at all for them, since they have always heard their words pronounced that way. But if you undertake to learn Chinese, you will have to try to remember each word with its tone.

The question is often asked whether Japanese belongs to the same language family as Chinese. The answer is an emphatic no. Japanese stands in a family by itself, with only Korean as a possible relative, though even this is doubtful. The Japanese written language uses Chinese pictographs and ideographs, having borrowed the writing system from China in the early Middle Ages, but even here there is a difference, because the Japanese devised two sets of syllabic characters out of special Chinese ideographs, and use them with a phonetic value, side by side with the other ideographs, either to explain them phonetically (just as when we write "$10—ten dollars"), or to supply endings on longer words (something Chinese never does, having no endings). The Japanese spoken language is not at all composed of words of only one syllable, and Japanese words are often quite long. Also, Japanese uses endings, to an even greater degree than we do. In Chinese, you cannot change "write" to "wrote," "have written," "shall write"; in Japanese you can. Furthermore, if you are speaking familiarly, "write" takes one form (*kaku*); but if you are speaking politely, it takes a different form (*kakimasu*).

The typical Japanese arrangement is consonant-vowel-consonant-vowel, while Chinese often ends its one-syllable words in -*n* or -*ng* (in some Chinese dialects, like Cantonese, you can also get -*t*, -*p*, -*k* at the end of a word). Japanese makes very little use of the tones of the voice to distinguish separate words. Lastly, the words of Chinese and Japanese are completely different, save where Japanese has borrowed Chinese words. For instance, the native Japanese word for "man" is *hito;* but you find also *jin*, borrowed from Chinese *jên*, and used especially in names of nationalities ("American" would be in Japanese *beikoku-jin*, or "riceland-man"). Japanese is the language of a population that is rapidly climbing toward the one hundred million mark, and since Korea was before the last war a Japanese possession, many of the thirty million Koreans speak Japanese.

At the southeastern tip of Asia is Malaya, the land that sends us most of the rubber for our automobile tires and a good deal of our tin. Malaya speaks a language that has no connection with any of those previously mentioned, but belongs to a vast family the rest of which appears in the islands of Indonesia (Java, Sumatra, Borneo, Celebes, Bali, etc.), the Philippines, New Zealand, Hawaii, the islands of Melanesia, Micronesia and Polynesia (Fiji, Solomons, Samoa, Tahiti, etc.). One language of this family, Malagasy, is spoken on the island of Madagascar, off the east African coast, and another appears on Easter Island, some 2,000 miles off the west coast of South America. All these island languages are called Malayo-Polynesian, and the number of their speakers is well over a hundred million.

The most important tongue of this group is Malay, which has been adopted as the official language of the new state of Indonesia, a country of over seventy million people, who speak different but related languages. Malay has been described as the world's easiest language, with no harsh sounds, no endings, no difficult rules of grammar. Before the last war the islands of Indonesia formed part of the Dutch colonial empire, and many Indonesians speak Dutch. The Malay that was even then current for trade purposes in the Dutch islands was written either with Arabic characters (most Indonesians being Moslems), or with Roman characters used with Dutch rules of spelling. The same Malay language in Malaya, a British possession, was written with English rules of spelling. This meant that the name of a city might appear as Surabaya (English spelling) or Soerabaja (Dutch spelling). The form of spelling used today for *Bahasa Indonesia* (the language of Indonesia) comes closer to the English than to the Dutch.

The Philippines speak a variety of languages related to Malay or Indonesian (Visaya, Ilocano, Igorote, etc.). One of these native tongues has been selected by the new Philippine government as the national language of the Philippines. Its name is Tagalog (with stress on *gal*, not on *tag*). But since the Philippines were first a Spanish, then an American possession, many Filipinos speak Spanish, or English, or both.

Hawaiian is the language of the Malayo-Polynesian family that we most often hear. We even know the meaning of many of its words: *lei* (the garland that the Hawaiians drape around your neck when you arrive or when you leave their islands); *hula hula* (the native dance); *luau* or *hukilau* (the picnic-style feast to which you are treated); *aloha oe* (the native farewell); and, of course, *ukulele*. A more difficult Hawaiian word is *humuhumunukunukua-puaa*, the very long name of a very small fish. Hawaiian is a soft, melodious tongue, with few consonants and many vowels. When a Hawaiian tries to say "Merry Christmas," he comes out with "Mele Kalikimaka," because in his language consonants can only come singly, and must be followed by vowels; also, there is no *r*, no *s*, no *t*, so *l* and *k* have to fill in.

Two large islands, Australia and Papua, or New Guinea, have native languages that do not seem related to the Malayo-Polynesian group, and which are difficult to classify, having been little studied. It is possible that they are related to one another. There are over one hundred such languages in Australia and on the smaller island of Tasmania, 130 or so in New Guinea. Their speakers are fewer than half a million all told.

Getting back to the mainland of Asia, the second greatest agglomeration of people in the world after China is India, a former British possession which has recently been subdivided into two independent states, India and Pakistan. The division was made along religious lines, the inhabitants of the new Indian state being for the most part of the Hindu faith, while those of Pakistan are Moslems. The population of India today is over the three hundred million mark, while Pakistan is rapidly approaching one hundred million. So far as languages are concerned, there are twenty-four major ones in the two countries and almost two hundred minor ones. On an Indian ten-rupee note (something like our $5 bill) the inscription appears in nine different languages. The languages of India are for the most part of two groups. In the south of the Indian Peninsula (called Dekkan, or "South," by the Indians) are languages of a family called Dravidian, spoken by over one hundred million people.

These Dravidian languages seem to be the earlier ones. The two most widely spoken are called Tamil and Telugu.

But at some time or other there came into India speakers of Indo-European languages, and these spread throughout the northern and central parts of the country until today they are spoken by over two hundred fifty million, or over two-thirds of the Peninsula's total population. Among these Indo-European tongues, the predominant ones are Hindustani and Bengali, two of the world's thirteen leading languages. Bengali, with about sixty million speakers, appears in the northeastern part of the Peninsula, around Calcutta, while Hindustani is used by over one hundred fifty million, and is rapidly spreading as the official tongue of both India and Pakistan. But here religion comes into play again. The Hindus of India call the language Hindi, and write it with characters that come down from Sanskrit, the ancient tongue of northern India and the earliest Indo-European language on record; but the Moslems of Pakistan call it Urdu, and write it with Arabic characters. There are other differences between Hindi and Urdu (Hindi, for instance, uses words from Sanskrit, to which Urdu prefers words from Arabic or Persian), but they are minor. As Hindi spreads in India, and Urdu in Pakistan, the combined Hindustani language tends more and more to become the national tongue of both countries.

But the other languages are still very much alive. In East Pakistan recently the Bengali speakers objected strenuously to being obliged to learn Urdu, while in India the experiment was made of carving out a new state, called Andhra, that would put together most of the speakers of Telugu. The two governments, however, are helped in their campaign for language unity by what is called "movie Hindustani," the Hindustani developed and used by the motion-picture industry that tries to reach the entire India-Pakistan market.

Hindustani is a fairly simple language, and shows very definitely that it belongs to our own Indo-European family. The Hindustani word for "fire," for instance, is *agni*, related to the Latin *ignis* from which we get "ignite" and "ignition." "Tooth" is *dant*, like our "dentist" and "dental." "Name" is *nam*. Since India and Pakistan were until recently British possessions, and still form part of the British Commonwealth of Nations, many million people in both countries speak English.

To the northwest of India and Pakistan is another Indo-European land, Iran, or, as it was formerly called, Persia. The Iranians and their neighbors, the Afghans, come close to thirty million, and their languages are closely linked to those of northern India, so much so that the name Indo-Iranian is applied to all of them. In the past, the Persian language was close to the Sanskrit, but when Persia turned Moslem, during the Middle Ages, many Arabic words came into it. Still, modern Persian shows its relationship to us by such words as *pidar*, "father"; *madar*, "mother"; *biradar*, "brother." It is one of the easiest languages in the world to learn, and one of the most majestic-sounding.

West of Iran lies Arabia, homeland of the Arabic language which today stretches across North Africa from Casablanca to Cairo, and south into the Sahara, as well as over the Middle East, in such countries as Syria, Jordan, Lebanon, Iraq and Saudi Arabia. Arabic is the greatest living Semitic tongue. While its speakers number about fifty million, it is the sacred language of Islam, which means that it affects or influences hundreds of millions of Moslems in central and east Africa, the Soviet Union, the Balkans, Iran, India, Pakistan, China, Malaya and Indonesia. The Moslems follow the dictates of the Koran, composed in Classical Arabic by Mohammed and his immediate followers, and since the Koran is read and recited in Moslem places of worship in much the same way that the Bible is used in our churches, practically all Moslems have some slight familiarity with the Arabic language, which has also contributed many words to their languages, and to our own (think of "algebra," "alcohol," "sofa," "magazine," "syrup").

Another important present-day Semitic language is Hebrew, used as a national tongue in Israel by over one million people, and as a religious tongue by Jews all over the world. Other Semitic tongues of antiquity were Akkadian, used by the Babylonians and Assyrians; Phoenician, spoken also by the Carthaginians, who ruled the Mediterranean before the Romans destroyed their power in the Punic Wars; and Aramaic or Syriac, the language spoken by the Jews at the time of Christ.

The Semitic languages are close to each other. The greeting "peace unto you" is common to both Arabic and Hebrew. It sounds *salaam aleikum* in the first, *shalom alekhem* in the second. "Father" is *ab* in Arabic, *av* in Hebrew (this, by the way, is where we get "abbot" and "abbey"). Some linguists believe that the Semitic languages may be linked also to Indo-European, but that is difficult to prove.

Chinese, Japanese, Hindustani, Bengali lie entirely in Asia. Malay is primarily an island language, but the islands of Indonesia, where it is most widely spoken, are geographically part of Asia. Arabic, while it started in Arabia, which is part of Asia, straddles the Suez Canal and may be said to be an Afro-Asiatic language. Actually, most of its speakers are in North Africa, scattered throughout Morocco, Algeria, Tunisia, Libya and Egypt, and while Arabic is not an originally African language, it happens to be the most widely spoken of all the languages of Africa.

Another Semitic language that seems to have had its origin in Arabia is the Amharic of Ethiopia, a tongue spoken by about six million people who form the predominant group of that East African land.

Throughout North Africa, and intermingled with Arabic and other Semitic languages, are tongues of the Hamitic stock, which are related to the Semitic — Berber, largely spoken in Morocco and Algeria, and said to be the descendant of the language of the ancient Numidians who were the allies of Rome in its struggles with Carthage; Tamashek, the tongue of the veiled Touaregs of the inner Sahara; and numerous others. In upper Egypt and Ethiopia are other large bodies of Hamitic speakers. The great Hamitic tongue of ancient times was the Egyptian of the hieroglyphs, which lasted for thousands of years, but finally gave way to Arabic. Its descendant, Coptic, is used as a religious language by African Christians.

South of the Sahara begin the tongues of the African Negroes, estimated to be over five hundred in number, and spoken by well over a hundred million people. They are subdivided into three groups—Sudanese-Guinean, Bantu, and Hottentot-Bushman. The first group appears along the Gulf of Guinea and in the interior of central Africa; among them are Ewe, Ibo and Hausa, the last of which is spoken in Nigeria by about fourteen million people. Speakers of Sudanese-Guinean tongues were brought to America in large numbers in colonial times, and have contributed to American English several words and expressions that are originally African, among them "okra," "gumbo," "goober" and "juke." On the coast of South Carolina some of the Negro inhabitants speak today a dialect called Gullah, which is a mixture of English and various African Negro languages of the Sudanese-Guinean family.

The Bantu group occupies the south central and southern portions of the African continent, and among these tongues is that of the Zulus, a proud and warlike race that fought both Boers and British in defense of their South African homeland. From the language of the Zulus we get terms like *impi*, "army," *inkoos* or *inkosi*, "chieftain," but also used in South Africa with the meaning of "thank you," and the second part of *knobkerry*, a war-club. Those of you who read the African adventure stories of Rider Haggard have undoubtedly picked up plenty of Zulu and Kaffir words.

One important Bantu language is the Swahili of the East African coast, spoken by over eight million people in Kenya, Tanganyika, Uganda, and other near-by lands. Swahili (also called Kiswahili) has been popularized by African safaris and African movies. It is said to be a compromise language devised by the Arab traders for communication with natives speaking a variety of Bantu languages, and among its words you may have come across *bwana* "sir," "master," *simba* "lion," *tembo* "elephant," and *mbogo* "buffalo." Among Bantu speakers are the Kikuyu, who have recently come into the public view by reason of the Mau Mau ("Hidden Ones"), a secret society that is giving the British authorities in Kenya a good deal of trouble.

In the African southwest is a group of tongues called Hottentot-Bushman, spoken for the most part by pygmies, which are quite different from the surrounding Bantu languages. One of their startling features is a series of click sounds, such as those produced when you smack your lips or cluck your tongue, and these are part of the regular language equipment of those languages. They strike us as strange because our consonant sounds are produced by driving out air, while these sounds are produced by taking in air. But when you stop to think, why shouldn't the sounds produced by sucking in air be utilized for language purposes, too?

Like the tongues of the American Indians, those of the African Negroes, the Australian natives and the inhabitants of the islands of the South Seas are for the most part unwritten. But missionaries first and scientists more recently have been busy devising written alphabets and forms for these languages, so that their speakers may become literate and join in the march of civilization. One man in particular, the Rev. Frank Laubach, has been responsible for bringing written forms to hundreds of these obscure languages of Asia, Africa, America and Oceania, and thereby making some of the blessings of modern civilization available to the people who speak them.

A couple of interesting things have been brought to light by an examination of the world's more remote languages. One is that there is no group of human beings, no matter how primitive or backward it may seem, that does not have a spoken language (many of them, on the other hand, did not have a written form until it was devised for them). This, in turn, would seem to show that the ability to speak is what truly distinguishes, on a material plane, the human from the animal world, and casts a new light upon the Biblical statement that "in the beginning was the Word, and the Word was with God, and the Word was God." What is human speaks. What is not human may produce various noises, but not true speech. Speech, in turn, is what enables us to reason in the true sense of the word, to establish symbols that are universally accepted and used within the group, and to derive general notions from individual examples.

Secondly, the study of obscure languages proves definitely that there is no such thing as a simple language, a language consisting only of grunts and groans and wheezes. Very often, the more primitive the society, the more complex and involved is the language. Each language is fully adequate to satisfy the needs of the group that uses it, and each language appears capable of infinite growth and development, as the civilization that uses it grows and expands.

This leads us to view the language of "primitive," "backward" groups with a respect that was not there before, and to realize that their speakers are human beings, exactly like ourselves, and that given the proper conditions of education and training, they probably can, in time, achieve the higher standards of civilization that have in part (and only in part) been achieved by us.

5 *One Language for Everybody?*

BACK IN OUR VERY FIRST CHAPTER, WE SAID there were two lessons to be learned from the Biblical story of the Tower of Babel. One was that without language there is no possibility of communication, of human cooperation, of civilization itself. The other is that even back in those early days people thought it would be desirable to have a single language, so that all would be able to understand one another. Then the cooperation that extends through only one group could be extended to all human groups throughout the world. All human beings would be able to work together, and all would be friends.

The people who wrote those early Biblical accounts thought in terms of the blessings that God had conferred upon men. Among those blessings was language, a language that all men would speak and understand. Men lost it through their own pride. Ever since then, men have been trying to regain it.

But pride still stands in the way. The speakers of each language say: "Yes, by all means let there be only one language, and let that language be ours!" But there are 2,796 languages, so there are, or at least there could be, 2,796 groups of people, each advocating the use of its own language for the entire world.

In reality, most groups, particularly the smaller ones, don't give the matter much thought. But speakers of the bigger, more important languages do, and each advances his own language as the logical candidate for the post. You will hear Americans and Britishers advocating English, Soviet citizens advocating Russian, Frenchmen advocating French, Germans German, and Spaniards and Spanish-Americans Spanish, to mention only a few.

There is not too much point to discussing their various and conflicting claims. Let us rather see whether it would be worth while to have a single world tongue. What would be the advantages of one language spoken and understood all over the world? Would the other languages have to disappear? Would the one language break up into new and different languages?

If you have ever traveled to a country of which you did not know the language, you will realize at once what a terrible disadvantage it is to be cut off from communication with those around you. You cannot make your wants known, ask for simple directions, present your point of view. The most you can do is use sign language, point to things, and pray that you will meet someone who speaks English.

But you need not travel to foreign lands. Right here in America you may run across people who don't speak English, and see how helpless they are, and what joy appears on their faces when they meet someone who can speak their tongue. Or you can go to the United Nations building in New York, and see how the representatives of sixty nations have to use interpreters and translators to be able to carry on their work, and how much time and labor are lost in the process of translating from one language to the others.

One can always learn other languages besides one's own. But it takes time, work and patience to learn even one foreign language, and when you have done it, if you come up against someone speaking one of the languages you haven't learned, you are just as helpless as though you didn't know any foreign language at all. It is far better to know English and French and Spanish than to know just English, but neither you nor anyone else will ever learn all of the 2,796 languages of the world; in fact, it is extremely unlikely that any one today knows thoroughly even the thirteen major world languages.

So a single tongue used all over the earth, side by side with each national language, for purposes of international communication, would be a great blessing to everybody. It would make it far easier to travel, trade, study, work, play. It would mean that you could communicate easily not only with the two hundred fifty million people who speak English, but with each and any of the world's two and a half billion inhabitants.

Has it ever been tried? Yes, on a limited scale. In the ancient world, once the Romans had gained control, two languages, Latin and Greek, were used side by side in all the countries that formed part of the Roman Empire. This was not the entire world, to be sure, but it was a very extensive section of the world that was known then. It embraced all of western and southern Europe, western Asia, and North Africa. It included the countries that are today Britain, France, Belgium, Holland, Spain, Portugal, Switzerland, Italy, Yugoslavia, Greece, Albania, Rumania, Bulgaria, Hungary, Turkey, Israel, Lebanon, Syria, Jordan, Egypt, Libya, Algeria, Tunisia, Morocco, as well as parts of Germany, Austria, Iran, and other countries.

Throughout this vast ancient world, Latin was the language of government and politics and military affairs, while Greek was the language of culture, and both Latin and Greek were used for commerce. Not everybody spoke both, of course, or even one of the two. But all people who were literate, and quite a few who were not, did, as proved by the fact that later on Latin became the universal popular spoken tongue of the western part of the Empire, and Greek of the eastern. This system of a universal language, or two universal languages, gave the Roman Empire tremendous advantages, which had been enjoyed by none of the countries that had previously existed. Roman officials and merchants could go from one end of the Empire to the other with the certainty that they would understand and be understood, from Britain to Mesopotamia, and from the Sahara to the German forests. Roman soldiers recruited from every province could get along together, by reason of Latin, the language of command.

When the Roman Empire fell, this universality did not cease all at once. The two languages, Latin and Greek, parted company, and each became universal in its own sphere. During the Middle Ages Latin finally broke up into the Romance languages, but Latin continued to be the language of the Western Church and the language of literacy and scholarship. Every one who wrote, wrote in Latin. The work of schools and universities was carried on exclusively in Latin, and students could go from Oxford in England to the Sorbonne in Paris, the University of Bologna in Italy, or that of Salamanca in Spain, or Heidelberg in Germany, or even Prague in Bohemia and Cracow in Poland, with the assurance that the lectures would be given in the same Latin tongue, regardless of the spoken language of the local population.

This universal use of Latin as a scholarly language began to wane around the year 1400, when the great national tongues, English, French, German, Italian and Spanish, began to come to the fore and be used more and more, largely because more and more people were learning to read and write. By the beginning of the seventeenth century, the various national languages had made such progress that Latin, though it continued to be used, and Greek, which had again come to the West in the fifteenth century, could no longer be described as universal languages.

At this point, it first began to occur to a few individuals that instead of using one or more existing languages for international purposes, people could perhaps build up a language for themselves that would belong to no one in particular, and for that very reason be acceptable to everybody. Initial attempts were made at constructing artificial languages, one of them by the great French philosopher Descartes, but they did not meet with much favor.

In the meantime, the habit began of using French as an international diplomatic tongue. France was at that time the most powerful and populated country in Europe, and this fact helped French to become established. But in the nineteenth century French began to lose ground to English and German, and in the twentieth Spanish, Russian and Chinese were entered in the race, by reason of their growing importance, attested by their official use in the United Nations councils.

Since the time of Descartes, it is estimated that no fewer than five hundred attempts have been made to create artificial languages for international use. The most successful by far has been Esperanto, a language constructed around the end of the nineteenth century by Dr. Zamenhof of Poland. Esperanto is a language that is extremely easy to learn and speak, with its words drawn mainly from English, German, the Romance languages, Latin and Greek. A more recent arrival on the international language scene is Interlingua, scientifically constructed by a group of language experts, ɔut of Latin, the Romance languages and English. But vhereas Esperanto has a large body of people who actually speak it scattered throughout the world, Interlingua has not yet achieved much popularity. If you should ever learn Esperanto, you will be able to recognize your fellow-Esperantists in any country by the little green star they wear in their lapel.

Along with the constructed languages, several national tongues have been considered for international use. Proposals have been advanced to make English, French, Spanish, Russian or Chinese the one language that everyone in the world will learn, along with his own tongue. A simplification of English, based on the use of fewer words to replace the many long words in our language, has been labeled Basic English and put forward as a possible world tongue. According to the Basic English scheme, a word like "selfish," which does not occur too often, would be replaced by a combination of four high-frequency words, "without thought of others," while "bush" would be replaced by "small tree." Churchill suggested during the war that Basic English might solve the world's communication problems, but of late the trend has been to use Basic English only as a device to start off foreigners who want to learn full English.

But here is where national pride comes into play. The main objection to the use of national language, ordinary, like full English, or modified, like Basic English, is that since the language reflects the habits of thought of the people who speak it, there would be a tendency for the world to become more and more Anglo-American if English were selected, or Soviet-like if Russian were selected, or French if French were chosen. The main objection to constructed languages, like Esperanto or Interlingua, is that they have not developed all the thought-carrying machinery and shades of meaning that natural languages have had a chance to work out for themselves over a period of many centuries; also, that the artificial languages presented so far lean too heavily in the direction of the western European and American nations, and carry too little in the way of Slavic, Asiatic and African words and habits of thought.

For the time being, this is as far as the international language question has gotten. International organizations, like the United Nations and UNESCO, which give their attention to problems that concern the entire world, have not made much progress in solving this one, though the establishment of an international language would help their work enormously.

The main difficulty lies in the choice of a language, national or constructed, to serve the world's needs. Once the choice were made, it would not be too difficult to put the international language into operation. It would be introduced into all the world's schools on equal terms with the individual national tongue of each country, and would be learned naturally by all growing boys and girls, with radio, TV and movies presenting part of their programs, all over the world, in the international tongue. Within twenty years, all people throughout the world who have access to schools, radio, TV or motion pictures would be speaking the international language along with their own. American children would grow up speaking English and international, Chinese children would speak Chinese and international, French children would have French and international, and this would mean that no matter what country you might visit, you would be able to talk easily and naturally to most of the inhabitants, by using the international language that you yourself would be able to speak as easily as you speak English.

The advantages would be many and varied. They would be reaped by business men, scientists, tourists, students, missionaries, people of all kinds and descriptions who have occasion to travel. Even without traveling, you could reap them at home, by being able to communicate with foreigners in our midst, and by having access to all kinds of programs and written materials that come from abroad.

One of the biggest advantages that would come from the creation and use of an international tongue is the spirit of greater friendliness that would prevail among the earth's peoples, because we are more inclined to be friendly with those we understand than with those we can't understand.

The chances that the international language would break up into new, different languages is slight. We are living in a historical period when communications are many and easy, and ease of communications leads to standardization of language rather than to its breaking up into dialects.

What would happen to the existing languages if an international language were to be adopted? For a long time, nothing at all. They would continue to be used within each country, side by side with the newcomer, in the same way that French and Flemish are used in Belgium, or French and English in the province of Quebec in Canada. The older people would not have the time or the inclination to learn the new international tongue, and they would go on using their present languages as long as they lived.

But as years and centuries go by, it would not be surprising if the national tongues got to be used less and less, and the international tongue more and more, because the international tongue could be used in all places, on all occasions, and to everybody, while the national languages would be restricted to their own areas. If this happened, it would mean that languages like English, French, German and Russian would eventually become like Latin and Greek—languages that one learns for purposes of culture and reading rather than for active spoken use. But this event would take place centuries from now, and by that time the spoken tongues of today would be so changed in any event that they would strike the person of that period as the language of Chaucer strikes us.

The international language problem is one to which we should at least devote some serious thought and attention. We may be called upon to solve it in our lifetime, and if this happens we ought to have some clear ideas on the subject.

Meanwhile, it is up to us to make the best use of what we have. We should cultivate our own language, and try to use it effectively, both when we speak and when we write. We should realize its vast importance in the world of today, and be proud of it, but at the same time realize also that nine out of ten people in the world speak something else and feel about their languages as we feel about ours. We should make an attempt to learn some of those languages, both for their own sake and for the light they shed on ours.

Above all, we should constantly keep in mind what a priceless gift language in general is, how it aids in all our activities and makes cooperation and civilization possible. Without language, we sink to the level of the animals. With language, there is practically no achievement that we need be afraid to try for. Language is the highest form of material power that mankind has been endowed with, and the foundation for all the other powers we have achieved or shall achieve in the future.

INDEX

INDEX